THE ART OF GETTING THINGS DONE

CLAY CLARK

The Art of Getting Things Done
ISBN: 978-0-999-86490-6
Copyright © 2018 by Clay Clark

Clay Clark Publishing

Published by Clay-Non-Deep-State Publishing
1100 Suite #100 Riverwalk Terrace
Jenks, OK 74037

CONTENTS

INTRODUCTION:

As a father of 5 kids, the founder of multiple multi-million dollar businesses (DJ Connection, EITR Lounge.com, EpicPhotos. com, MakeYourLifeEpic.com, etc.), the owner of multiple existing businesses and the host of the daily 2 hour ThriveTime Business Coach Radio Show and Podcast, I am often asked, "how do you get so much done during your day?" This book was written to answer that question pragmatically and succinctly. I am writing this book to help you dramatically improve your ability to manage your day and to get stuff done. My friend, if we all have the same 24 hours in every day, how is that some people seem to get so much more done during their days than everyone else? It all comes down to time management and in this book, I will teach you the specific non deep-state tactics and systems that I and many successful entrepreneurs use to get things done on a daily basis.

Phil Pressey (former member of the Boston Celtics)

and my father, Thom Clark.

SPECIAL DEDICATION:

....

I dedicate this book to my Dad. My dad, who lost his battle with

ALS (Lou Gherig's disease in 2016), showed me through both

his actions and words how important it is to remember how

precious every moment of every day of life is.

Dad, I miss you and I hated watching your body die,

but I know your soul lives on.

NOTABLE QUOTABLE

"This is the day the Lord has made; we will rejoice and be glad in it."

- PSALM 118:24

(From that controversial book called The Bible.)

CLAY CLARK TRANSLATION

"It's profound every day that you are above the ground."

When my dad called me I was sitting in my white Hummer at our 1100 Riverwalk Terrace ThriveTimeShow.com World Headquarters office. Dad told me that test results were finally in and that he had been diagnosed with ALS "Lou Gehrig's Disease" (amyotrophic lateral sclerosis, the progressive neurodegenerative disease that affects nerve cells in the brain and the spinal cord. A-myo-trophic comes from the Greek language. "A" which means no. "Myo" refers to muscle, and "Trophic" means nourishment, which in total, means "No muscle nourishment"). Neither of us were Greek scholars, but we both knew that this new diagnosis was the beginning of the end for him and soon he would die of suffocation after his body would gradually lose the ability first to walk, then to talk and then to ultimately breathe.

I have never cried like I did when my Dad told me, "I'm sorry son." And I don't know why he was saying, "sorry." It wasn't his fault, but yet he said, "I'm sorry son." I'll never forget that statement. I told my Dad I loved him, and then I put the phone down, wiped the tears out of my eyes and went back to inside the building and back to work, because work is my worship and my vocation (which in Latin means "calling"). For me work has always been a vocation and vocation has been work.

Then on the way home after I had completed a full day's work it hit me again, but this time it was heavier, more damning and more unsettling.

So heavy in fact this time that I couldn't drive my car because I was shaking so much while I cried. To prevent myself from killing someone on the road, I had to pull over just 2 miles past the office on the right side of the entrance to the Creek Turnpike.

I cried and I cried until I mentally accepted the finality of my father's death sentence. This has always been how I deal with the horrible things that happen to me everyday. I always embrace the worst case scenario, and Dad's suffering was this worst case scenario. I had to come to terms with the fact that his eventual death was actually going to be a release, but that the process of him dying was going to be awful. I knew that I would eventually have to watch my Dad die in front of me, but that I was also blessed to know that his life was going to be ending soon and that it was up to me as to whether I was going to make the time to invest into our relationship or not. On September 5th (also the same day that our Radio Show was first aired during its prime-time noon slot) Dad went to be with the Lord and he was freed of his decaying earthly body.

It was also on this day that Dad taught me that final time management lesson that I needed to learn.

the help of partner and friend Jonathan Barnett who is the CEO of the 300 + franchisee location (OxiFresh.com Carpet Cleaning Brand).

 www.EpicPhotos.com - One of the nation's largest wedding photography businesses at the time that Clay sold it. His company won TheKnot.com "Best Photography Award" in 2011, 2013, 2014, 2015, 2016, 2017 and became a member of TheKnot.com's "Best of Weddings" Hall of Fame.

 www.MakeYourLifeEpic.com - The marketing firm he has built currently is one of Oklahoma's largest and most established marketing firms, having been in business since 2006. The company works with small and medium-sized companies who produce a total gross revenue of over $600 million per year.

 Party Perfect Rentals now known as **www.PartyProRents.com** Clay grew Party Perfect Rentals before selling it to the company that has now become Oklahoma's largest party rental company.

www.ThriveTimeShow.com - This company is the world's most effective business coaching program for small and medium sized business owners. This business is Clay's passion and his heart song. We are convinced that he will die while still business coaching because he never gets tired of seeing the positive impact the having both financial and time freedom can have on a person and their family.

MOVE #1

YOU MUST BLOCK OUT 1 HOUR OF
MORNING PLANNING TIME IF YOU
ARE AMBITIOUS.
(ALSO KNOWN AS QUIET TIME, PLANNING TIME,
OR PRAYER TIME.)

NOTABLE QUOTABLE

"By failing to prepare, you are preparing to fail."

- BENJAMIN FRANKLIN

(One of the Founding Fathers of the United States. Franklin was a renowned polymath and a leading author, printer, political politician, postmaster, scientist, inventor, humorist, civic activist, statesman, and diplomat. As a scientist, he was a major figure in the history of physics for his discoveries and theories regarding electricity. As an inventor, he is known for the lightning rod, bifocals, and the Franklin stove, among other inventions. He is a man who got a lot of stuff done.)

If you are going to become successful you must be good at designing and planning successful and productive days, and this is not possible if you do not BLOCK OUT THE SPECIFIC TIME to plan out your days. I call this time my daily "meta time." The word meta, comes from the Greek word that stands for "above and beyond."

To become successful you must schedule a specific time and place to do your meta-time. If you don't do this you will never become a proactive person.

I would challenge you here and now to write out the answers to the following questions for your betterment:

 Where will you do your daily planning?

_____

 When will you do your daily planning?

_____

 What do you need to have available to daily execute

your schedule & planning? (computer, pens, paper,

music, a desk, beer jerky, etc.)

_____

MOVE #2

PURPOSELY DECIDE WHAT AND WHO
YOU ARE GOING TO SAY "NO" TO.

NOTABLE QUOTABLE

"People think focus means saying yes to the thing you've got to focus on. But that's not what it means at all. It means saying no to the hundred other good ideas that there are. You have to pick carefully. I'm actually as proud of the things we haven't done as the things I have done. Innovation is saying no to 1,000 things."

- STEVE JOBS

(The man who personally lead the charge to make personal computers that non-nerds could use, the man who co-founded Apple, the man who introduced the first 100% digitally animated box office success story (Toy Story) when he was the CEO of the company. The man who revolutionized the music industry with the iPod and iTunes. The man who introduced the iPad tablet technology to the planet and the man who introduced the game-changing smartphone, the iPhone to the planet. He was a dude who got things done.)

Regardless of how most people feel about it, success requires trade-offs and your network is determined by your net worth. Thus, you must decide specifically right now what you are going to stop doing and who you are going to stop hanging out with. You can't become successful if you are still watching 5 hours of TV per day. As an example, on a daily basis I block out at least 1 person from calling, texting, or emailing me. Why? Because the former business partner, who could never get their stuff done, will never stop trying to have one more "quick call" to try to make things right.

Extended family members who I've kicked out of my life for bringing their horrible lifestyles into my living room don't deserve my time. You must value your life enough to refuse to let other people waste it. It's not possible to become successful if you are spending every waking hour of your day surrounded by lazy and negative people. I promise you, the people that you are around will become your "new normal," because they will influence your mindset and they will cause you to lose.

Whatever the majority of your friends deem acceptable will become "ok" and "acceptable" to you. I would challenge you here and now to write out the answers to the following questions for your betterment:

(?) Who do you need to stop spending time with?

_____

_____

_____

(?) What activities do you need to stop participating in?

_____

_____

_____

(?) What organizations do you need to stop investing time in?

_____

_____

_____

(?) List out the ways you wasted time during

the past 7 days and stop doing these things:

_____

_____

_____

18 years later, I actually enjoy doing sales calls because it's fun doing something that you are good at and that you can earn money doing.

I would challenge you here and now to write out the answers to the following questions for your betterment:

(?) What needs to be done for your business that you have been putting off?

_____

(?) Who do you need to fire right now?

_____

(?) Who do you need to hire right now?

_____

(?) What expense do you need to cut right now?

_____

(?) What difficult conversation do you need to have this week?

_____

(?) What person do you need to cut out of your life?

_____

(?) What vaping Obama voter do you need to stop listening to?

_____

MOVE #6

STOP LAMENTING ABOUT THINGS.

NOTABLE QUOTABLE

"You don't need more time, you just need to decide."

- SETH GODIN

(The man who used his personal life savings of $20,000 to start Seth Godin Productions, which was a book publishing business. He then teamed up with Mark Hurst to found Yoyodyne which was sold to Yahoo! For $30 million. He is the best selling author of numerous books including, Tribes, Linchpin, The Purple Cow, etc. He gets things done.)

It's important that you give yourself time to grieve when you experience a loss, a rejection or feel sad, but I recommend that you never spend more than 1 hour lamenting over anything, EVER. My Dad pitched in the 1965 Little League World Series. He delivered pizzas in his 30's to put food on our table, he taught me the importance of comedy by forcing me to watch the *Blues Brothers*, *Animal House*, *The Jerk*, *Airplane* and countless other comedies, and my dad (Thom Clark) tragically died of ALS (Lou Gehrig's Disease).

It might sound harsh, but I will never get over watching him die in front of me and yet you will probably forget that you even read my Dad's name (Thom Clark) 2 months from now. 12 months from now, most of the people who attended my Dad's funeral will no longer think about his life on a consistent basis. 70 years from now, no one will even remember my Dad's life, because I will be 107 (most likely dead) years old and my kids won't bring his name up in conversation on a consistent basis.

700 years from now, no one in my family will even care that my Dad ever existed for the same reason that I cannot remember my own Grandmother's full name (Dorothy Clark is all I can remember).

My friend you must decide here and now to get over whatever it is that happened to you in the past.

I would challenge you here and now to write out the answers to the following questions for your betterment:

 What is something that I need to get over that I am still emotionally lamenting?

_____

 Who is a person that I need to get over that I am still emotionally lamenting over?

_____

Who hurt me that I need to get over that I am still

emotionally lamenting over?

_____

 Who is a perpetually vaping Obama voter that can't stop

getting divorced that you need to quit responding to??

_____

to business law and they are the legal team of choice for other top ministry leaders I respect.

I pay a personal trainer to advise me on nutrition and working out because he has spent a disproportionate amount of his time learning how to become the best physical fitness trainer possible. If you insist on becoming an expert at everything, you will fail and it will be your fault. I would challenge you here and now to write out the answers to the following questions for your betterment:

What are the areas of your life that you are struggling the most in?

_____

_____

Who clearly knows more than you about the areas of life that you are struggling in the most?

_____

_____

How much is it costing you to not know what you are doing in these given areas: your marriage, your sales, your accounting, your search engine optimization ranking, etc.?

a. _____

_____

b. _____

_____

c. _____

_____

d. _____

_____

e. _____

_____

MOVE #8

CUT NEGATIVE TEAM MEMBERS AND FAMILY MEMBERS OUT OF YOUR LIFE.

"BUT I WANTED TO BE LIKED AND LOVED BY EVERYBODY SO I WOULD NEVER KICK A PERSON OUT OF MY LIFE."

The passive mindset that allowed the Nazi party to convince the "weak-ass, herd mentality sheeple living in Germany at the time that it was ok to separate the Jews from the Germans.

NOTABLE QUOTABLE

"A person's success in life can usually be measured by the number of uncomfortable conversations he or she is willing to have."

- TIM FERRISS

(The best-selling author, investor and life-optimizer whose podcast The Tim Ferriss Show which has over 200+ million downloads.)

I don't care whether you have a million dollars or seven dollars, it's hard to enjoy yourself or get anything done when you are surrounded by the momentum-killing negative feedback from negative, or simply ignorant, team or family members. The fact that you were born in the same home, and attended the same school as these people does not forever damn you to a life of jackassery, negative conversations, and the constant barrage of unwanted feedback.

I would challenge you here and now to write out the answers to the following questions for your betterment:

(?) What family members do you need to draw the line with and to give them a final warning?

_____

(?) What family members do you need to cut out of your life?

_____

(?) What negative team members do you need to cut out of your life?

_____

(?) What negative, Obama-voting, vaping people do you need to stop responding to?

_____

NOTABLE QUOTABLE

"He who walks with the wise will become wise, but the companion of fools will be destroyed. Walk with the wise and become wise, for a companion of fools suffers harm. Walk with the wise and become wise; associate with fools and get in trouble. Whoever walks with the wise becomes wise, but the companion of fools will suffer harm."

- PROVERBS 13:20

MOVE #9

GET YOUR E-MAIL INBOX
TO ZERO DURING THE MORNING AND
STOP CHECKING IT INCESSANTLY
DURING THE DAY.

NOTABLE QUOTABLE

"You can't run your life from your email inbox."

- CLAY CLARK

Over the years I've had the opportunity to free up thousands of entrepreneurs from the mental disorder that I call "**monkey brain**" this is caused by incessantly checking your email, text messages, voicemail, and social media updates over and over in an addictive manner. My friend, you cannot control who sends you an email, but you can control how often you check that inbox. You must get your work email out of your personal computer and your phone. It's just not possible to efficiently respond to work-related emails that keep flying into your phone, you can really only be a victim who just knows that you are being mentally bombarded with emails that you don't have the time to respond to right now. This will ruin your time away from work, and this will keep you from ever being mentally engaged away from work.

You must learn to get your inbox down to zero (delete and sort all emails before 9:00 AM) each morning before you start your work day and then must discipline yourself to not check your e-mail during the day if you want to be a productive person. I would challenge you here and now to write out the answers to the following questions for your betterment:

? How many times per day are you currently checking your email?

_____

? What is the minimum number of times that you need to check your email during the day (9:00 AM, 4:00 PM, etc.?)

_____

? How many times per day are you checking Telegram to read posts of an Obama supporter who can't stop vaping and getting divorced?

_____

MOVE #10

STOP ARGUING ABOUT
RELIGION.

NOTABLE QUOTABLE

"The only way to get the best of an argument is to avoid it."

- DALE CARNEGIE

(The best-selling author of How to Win Friends and Influence People.)

It's odd, disturbing, sad or just weird, but even the Christian religion has now been broken in 21,000 denominations (World Christian Encyclopedia, David A. Barrett; Oxford University Press, 1982). Why? It's because pastors, monks, priests and theologians who have devoted their entire lives to studying the Christian religion could not agree on an interpretation of scripture and they refused to quit arguing about it until their church finally had to be split apart. My friend, I am a huge fan of the New England Patriots for all the reasons that you probably hate them, but that's okay and I am fine with that.

However, if I spent the remainder of this book or the remainder of my life trying to convince you that they are truly "America's Team", I could not win the argument. Furthermore, one out of four of you would say that the National Football League is not even worth watching because the players kneel during the playing of the National Anthem. Then one quarter of you would try to convince me that soccer was the best sport in the world. So, instead of wasting both my time and yours, we won't discuss the value of the National Football League or the dominance of the New England Patriots. My friend, use this example and save yourself time and energy by simply refusing to argue about religion.

I would challenge you here and now to write out the answers to the following questions for your betterment:

 Who have you been arguing religion with?

_____

 How many hours have you spent arguing about religion?

_____

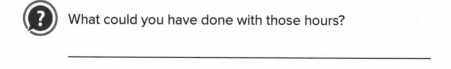 What could you have done with those hours?

_____

MOVE #11

STOP ARGUING ABOUT POLITICS.

BONUS TIP

Want to waste time? Ask a Republican and a Democrat to agree on how to balance a budget and make it a rule that they can't stop arguing until both parties agree.

NOTABLE QUOTABLE

"People's minds are changed through observation and not through argument."

- WILL ROGERS

(A stage and motion picture actor, vaudeville performer, American cowboy, humorist, newspaper columnist, and social commentator. Will was a cowboy who got things done.)

For some of you this will be really hard because you are having a TRUMP-tastic time reading this book, or because you believe that President Obama was the first REAL President. Either way, half of the United States disagrees with you, so in terms of getting things done, I would encourage you to not bring up politics when possible. Certain people believe that we should raise taxes and take care of every sob story and person who refuses to work out there and other people believe that we should overthrow the government and live a completely Libertarian lifestyle buried in a bunker somewhere while clinging to our guns and gold. I would challenge you here and now to write out the answers to the following questions for your betterment:

 Who do you argue politics with the most?

_____

 How many hours have you spent arguing about politics?

_____

 What could you have done with those hours?

_____

MOVE #12

FOCUS ON WHAT YOU
CAN CONTROL.

NOTABLE QUOTABLE

"Waste no more time arguing about what
a good man should be. Be one."

- MARCUS AURELIUS

*(A Roman emperor from 161 to 180, who ruled jointly with Lucius Verus
until Verus' death in 169 and jointly with his son, Commodus, from 177. Marcus
was a Roman Emperor who got stuff done.)*

People whose attitudes and emotions are controlled by other people, the news, the weather, and outside forces really struggle through life. Each new day introduces you to new people with new negative personalities and new circumstances. If you are depressed because somebody attacked your character, life is going to be really hard for you.

Regardless of whether people are nice to you or not, you just have to shut the hell up, get to work and get your things done. I would challenge you here and now to write out the answers to the following questions for your betterment:

(?) What people do you currently allow to make you the most unproductive?

_____

(?) Determine here and now that you will have your most productive days when the negative people are at their worst.

a. Name _____

b. Date _____

c. Signature _____

MOVE #13

BE A LOVER AND NOT A FIGHTER
WHEN POSSIBLE.

NOTABLE QUOTABLE

"We have plenty of opportunities to get angry, stressed or offended. But when you spend your day on these negative emotions it wastes your life and your time."

- CLAY CLARK

For me, the concept of being a lover and not a fighter has always very hard for me to grasp. When somebody wrongs you, screws you, or takes advantage of you, you must stop and consider Matthew 5:10 from that controversial book called *The Bible*. It states, "Blessed are those who are persecuted

because of righteousness, for theirs is the kingdom of heaven."
My friend, if you stand up for anything, you will be attacked and you
cannot lose countless hours and years fighting to right every wrong;
sometimes you just have to let it go. I would challenge you here and
now to write out the answers to the following questions for your betterment:

 In what areas of your life do you just need to "let it go?"

_____

 Who in your life has screwed you over the most?

_____

 What can you do to expedite the ending of the doom loop
that is being created as a result of you remaining in
constant communication with the person that has
wronged you?

_____

 How much time have you spent explaining to an Obama
voter who can't stop vaping and getting divorced that you
are not a member of the Illuminati?

_____

MOVE #14

WORK VIA
APPOINTMENT ONLY.

NOTABLE QUOTABLE

"You can't build a reputation on what you are going to do, or what you believe others should have done."

- CLAY CLARK

If you have ever tried to hire a contractor, invite friends out to dinner, or close a deal with a potential client, you will appreciate this move. It's SUPER IMPORTANT that henceforth you only work by appointment. When you ask people, "What specific time do you want to meet about that?" something magical happens, it forces them to make a decision. However, if you never ask people for a specific time to meet or go out for dinner, you will be caught in a constantly unproductive, soul-sucking and stupid game I call "THE DOOM LOOP OF PHONE TAG HELL."

You know what this means. It's where you call them and they call you and you keep running into each other at church each Sunday saying something bogus like, "Hey we should get together sometime" but you never do because neither party is forced to set a specific time. When either party agrees to a specific time, the result is amazing. One of two things will take place: either you immediately discover their true objection, or you will book a specific time. Either way, it will free up your schedule and will help you get more things done faster.

I would challenge you here and now to write out the answers to the following questions for your betterment:

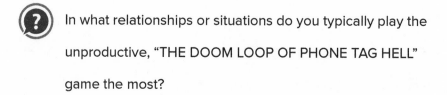 In what relationships or situations do you typically play the unproductive, "THE DOOM LOOP OF PHONE TAG HELL" game the most?

_____

How many times have you gone around and around with this other party saying, "I'll call you back."

_____

MOVE #15

CREATE ONE EMAIL INBOX.

NOTABLE QUOTABLE

"Simplicity is the ultimate sophistication."

- LEONARDO DA VINCI

(An Italian Renaissance polymath whose areas of interest included inventing, painting, sculpting, architecture, science, music, mathematics, engineering, literature, anatomy, geology, astronomy, botany, writing, history, and cartography. He was a dude that knew what to do to get things done.)

You will struggle to be productive if you have 3 different email inboxes to check every day. For the sake of your time I am not going to belabor this point because I know that you know that I am correct on this idea. Just have one e-mail for your life and you will become more productive and you will get more things done. I would challenge you here and now to write out the answers to the following questions for your betterment:

 What email address do you need to blow up?

_____

 How many unread (un-deleted) emails do you have?
(Hint: I have zero after every morning)

_____

MOVE #16

DETERMINE TO GET YOUR
ACTION ITEMS DONE EVERY DAY,
NO MATTER WHAT.

NOTABLE QUOTABLE

"You either pay now or pay later with just about every decision you make about where and how you spend your time."

- CLAY CLARK

Our world is filled with unproductive drifters who hide behind the statement, "To me, relationships are what really matter the most." These people will label productive people as "Alphas," "workaholics," "OCD," and "selfish," but the reality is that most people are perpetually disorganized, distracted and they work for "Type-A Workaholics" like me. Bottom line if you want to be successful you must ordain your destiny by designing each day and committing to complete all of the action items on your list come hell or high water.

? In what areas of your life are you drifting (not getting your to do list done)?

_____

? What is preventing you from getting your daily action items done?

_____

? What do you need to pull out of your daily schedule to get your daily action items done?

_____

MOVE #17

FIRE UNHAPPY PEOPLE AND
CONTRACTORS.

NOTABLE QUOTABLE

"We believe that it's really important to come up with core values that you can commit to. And by commit, we mean that you're willing to hire and fire based on them. If you're willing to do that, then you're well on your way to building a company culture that is in line with the brand you want to build."

- TONY HSIEH

(The man who sold his first company, LinkExchange, to Microsoft for $265 million in 1999, and then went on to get more things done by becoming CEO of Zappos shoe company.)

I have had the opportunity to meet with multiple billionaires who have told me, "Hire character and train skill." At first, I thought, "How is this possible? Don't they know I own an entertainment company?" I originally thought, "Yeah, but my business is different!" However, over time I began to realize that the billionaires were right. You can teach almost anyone any skill, but you can't teach unhappy people to be happy.

MOVE #18

(THE LONGEST CHAPTER OF THIS BOOK,
BECAUSE IT'S ABOUT FEELINGS)

AVOID DISCUSSIONS PERTAINING TO HOW PEOPLE FEEL WHEN POSSIBLE.

This won the award
for being the

**"CHAPTER WITH
THE MOST WORDS"**

So that this chapter wouldn't
feel bad for standing out from
all the other chapters.

NOTABLE QUOTABLE

"Quit debating optimism and pessimism.
Just get it done."

- CLAY CLARK

During your work day, if you want to accomplish your goals it is super important to avoid conversations about how you and I feel about the both the task at hand and about how we "feel" in general. My friend, both you and I have gone through something or are going to go through something that is horrific and it's hard to get much done if we only work hard on the days where we all feel motivated.

It's called discipline. It's called rigor. It's called will-power and the people with both self-discipline and will-power most often win and the slackers who lose will want you to know why you failed to motivate them which is why they believe they failed to hit the deadline or to get something done.

We have all had bad experiences happen to us and if asked how we feel, we could all drum up an endless variety of excuses and justifications for not feeling motivated enough to do what we need to do. As of the time I'm writing this book (age 37) the following horrible things have happened to me and I'm sure that if I live long enough more terrible things will happen to me:

1. I stuttered as a kid and was bullied because of it.

2. My best-friend was killed in an auto accident when we were college roommates.

3. My son was born blind.

4. My wife had a miscarriage.

5. My Dad died of ALS.

6. I've been screwed by countless business partners and employees.

My biggest personal potential excuse for not becoming successful, that I can think of, is being molested as a kid. Growing up, kids chose to pick on me because I stuttered so severely; they were merciless. They would shove me into walls, push me down, hit me when we would play touch football, and they would constantly call me, "C, cuh, cuh, cuh Clayton." They would introduce me to others as though that was my actual name. All I wanted was a friend. One day a neighbor kid (not the Guthmann family kids and or the White family kids), who was much older than me, invited me to his house. I was excited about the invitation because I had never been invited over to his house before. But this was not the invitation I was expecting. He and his sister molested me, and it became a reoccurring abuse.

Q

DEFINITION

Molest - Definition 1 - To annoy, disturb, or persecute
especially with hostile intent or injurious effect.
The zookeeper warned the visitors not to molest the animals.
Definition 2 - To make annoying sexual advances to;
especially : to force physical and usually sexual contact on.

The molestation that I endured was sexual and that is all the detail that I want to provide. After weeks of abuse, I eventually refused to go over to their house, and then the real bullying started. It resulted in me eventually trying to stand up to the teenage boy (who was ½ of the problem), in response, he punched me. His punch hurt me physically, but the finality of the punch forever changed the way that I see the world.

At that moment in time, I remember mentally committing to withdrawing contact with most humans. I decided that I would spend my time drawing pictures instead. As a result, I became an above average artist, and developed two superpowers that very few other people have:

Superpower #1, I do not need human interaction or encouragement EVER.

Superpower #2, I can focus for hours, weeks and months in a row on a subject without needing to take a break to socialize with other people because to me socializing represents potential danger.

Just in the way that most people fear touching a hot pan, I fear conversing with most people because I do not want to be burned again.

Often times on weekends I will not speak a single word to other humans other than my wife and kids because I do not want or need human interaction. As I have grown older, these superpowers have benefited me more and more.

The following celebrities and successful people have fought through tremendous adversity, but yet they went on to do something productive with their lives:

 Benjamin Franklin - Benjamin's family could not afford to send him to formal schooling, so he was only able to attend one year of formal education. Then his father sent him off to be trained and apprenticed by his older brother who published the paper, the New England Courant. Because Benjamin was ambitious and his brother (James) would not allow him to write for the paper he wrote letters to the editor under the pen name of Mrs. Dogood. Soon the articulate and witty letters became famous throughout Boston. When Benjamin finally told James that he was the one writing the famous letters to the editor, he was beat him severely.

Carlos Santana - He was sexually abused as a child. In 2003, *Rolling Stone magazine* listed Santana at number 20 on their list of the 100 Greatest Guitarists of All Time. He has won 10 Grammy Awards and three Latin Grammy Awards.

Chris Gardner - Before becoming a successful entrepreneur, Chris Gardner and his son once lived on the street and would often spend their nights sleeping inside of subway bathrooms. His life story was later turned into the movie,

starring Will Smith titled, *The Pursuit of Happyness*.

Joyce Meyer - She was sexually abused as a child. In 2005, *Time Magazine's* "25 Most Influential Evangelicals in America" ranked Meyer as 17th.

Maya Angelou - She was raped by her very own mother's boyfriend at the age of eight. She went on to receive over 50 honorary degrees and to become one of the most renowned poets of her time. In fact she was asked by the President of the United States, (Bill Clinton), to speak at his inauguration on the 20th of January, in 1993.

Although you and I are both flawed individuals and nobody is perfect, as a business coach I have found that the biggest struggles that most people deal with while building a business can be summarized as:

- » Not Knowing WHAT to do
- » Choosing to NOT DO WHAT YOU KNOW YOU NEED to do

NOTABLE QUOTABLE

"They were using this question as a trap, in order to have a basis for accusing him. But Jesus bent down and started to write on the ground with his finger. When they kept on questioning him, he straightened up and said to them, "Let any one of you who is without sin be the first to throw a stone at her." Again he stooped down and wrote on the ground. At this, those who heard
began to go away one at a time, the older ones first, until only Jesus was left, with the woman still standing there.
Jesus straightened up and asked her, "Woman, where are they?

Has no one condemned you?" "No one, sir," she said.
Then neither do I condemn you," Jesus declared.
"Go now and leave your life of sin."

- JOHN 8: 6-11

(From that controversial book known as The Bible that only a bigot who is dumb enough to cling to his guns, gold and religion would read...I guess I might be a bigot.)

As a business coach, I get to see people for who they really are, which often is amazingly inspiring and, unfortunately at times, it can be depressing, if I allow myself to focus on how I feel. I have witnessed many people and their lack of diligence up close, and because I have simply grown numb to most human interaction, it never really bothers me.

 For example, having worked with many clients for years, I've learned that Doctor Joe Lai is a great person and I can sincerely say that I love him as a friend. Our relationship started out as that of his business Kirkpatrick and Lai Orthodontics (KLOrtho.com) simply being a client.

 During my time working with Coach Don Calvert, I've learned that Don is a super diligent person who cares deeply about the students that he mentors at his business Score Basketball (ScoreBBall.com).

Also as a business coach and as a member of numerous church congregations I have learned first hand the following things:

1. PASTOR DAVID GROTHE -

Is a great man, committed husband, and a loving father. He loves music and is a man who Vanessa and I were honored to have as our Pastor and officiate our wedding. I wonder why his churches always grow.

2. PASTOR B (REAL STORY) -

Is a man who has never really stopped having extra-marital affairs, he has just been caught a few times. I wonder why his church stopped growing?

3. PASTOR C (REAL STORY) -

Is a man who never really believed in *The Bible* and later came out and actually told his congregation that he didn't believe in *The Bible*. I wonder why his church fell apart.

5. PASTOR D (REAL STORY) -

Is a man who had to be forcibly removed from the school his father started as a result of spending copious amounts of donated money on himself and his multi-millionaire lifestyle. I wonder why his university was failing?

Although being picked on as a kid did impact me in negative ways, it has also benefited me greatly. Today, having the ability to not need human interaction has provided an uncanny ability to focus in a way that most people just can't keep up with.

I can now write entire books during a weekend (like this one). I was able to deep dive in a magnificently obsessive way to create the world's best and most affordable search engine optimization system. I can read five 300+ page books in a weekend and I can do intense research on subjects for hours and hours on end. However, I struggle to hold a social conversation with people for even a few seconds. For me going to The Olive Garden, The Mall or most churches is more stressful than I can possibly explain with words.

NOTABLE QUOTABLE

"I pay no attention whatever to anybody's praise or blame.

I simply follow my own feelings."

- WOLFGANG MOZART

(Born in Salzburg, he showed incredible ability from a very young age. By the age of five he was already proficient on both the keyboard and the violin. At the age of 17, he was a paid musician at the Salzburg court. He began composing music at the age of five. However, he decided to leave in search of a better opportunity. Throughout his career he had very little financial success, but yet he achieved tremendous fame and wrote epic and now famous symphonies, concerts, and operas.)

I grew up not caring about what people thought about me because if I did value what they thought about me, I would have been chronically depressed. Even my neighbors mercilessly mocked me, and when they weren't, I was being molested. Today, all I care about are facts and what the proven "best practice systems" are. I am relentlessly future-focused and solution oriented. My friend, God has a plan for your life and there are Pastors, counselors, friends and significant others out there that want to hear your story, but if you want to get things done in the workplace you cannot spend your time asking people how they feel or worrying about how you feel. You get paid for the value you bring to every hour, but unless you are a psychologist, a pastor, a comedian, or some art-related profession, you simply need to not worry about how you feel while at work.

NOTABLE QUOTABLE

"You can't get much done in life if you only work
on the days when you feel good."

- JERRY WEST

*(A retired professional basketball player who played his entire professional
career for the Los Angeles Lakers of the National Basketball Association
(NBA). Throughout his career he was nicknamed, "Mr. Clutch." He had an
ability to always hit the "big shot", in fact, he hit the buzzer-beating 60-foot
shot that tied Game 3 of the 1970 NBA Finals against the New York Knicks;
The NBA logo is in reference to his silhouette.)*

I would challenge you here and now to write out the answers to the following questions for your betterment:

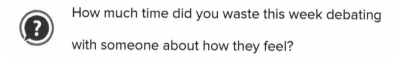 How much time did you waste this week debating with someone about how they feel?

_____

How often do you find yourself arguing with the people in your life about feelings?

_____

How often do you find yourself debating with an Obama voter who can't stop vaping and getting divorced about not being a member of the Illuminati?

_____

MOVE #19

AGREE ON A UNIVERSAL FILE NAMING
SYSTEM AND FORBID THE USE
OF ACRONYMS.

To scale a business, you must teach your team to name files correctly and consistently. If you don't do this on a very basic and fundamental level, you cannot scale a business.

If everyone is running around constantly asking where this file or that file is saved, you will spend your entire day reacting to sincere people on your team who can't find the basic answers to their routine daily questions. If you are ever going to scale your business and get things done quickly, you must stay organized and be fastidious about keeping your file naming system consistent. I would challenge you here and now to write out the answers to the following questions for your betterment:

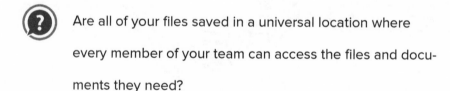 Are all of your files saved in a universal location where every member of your team can access the files and documents they need?

_____

Are all of your files, photos and important documents perpetually backed up on a daily basis?

_____

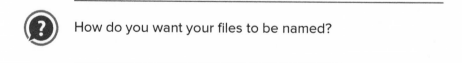 How do you want your files to be named?

_____

MOVE #20

SET UP CALL RECORDING
IN YOUR OFFICE.

NOTABLE QUOTABLE

"Only the paranoid survive."

- ANDY GROVE

(The Hungarian-born American success story was an engineer. One of the leading researchers and developers in the semiconductor industry. After he was able to finish schooling he was one of the founders of Intel and was the Chief Executive Officer. Many credit him for essentially creating Silicon Valley as we know it today.)

If you are not recording the calls of your business team, you are being screwed and your team is doing a bad job - guaranteed. Without exception, every single entrepreneur that I have worked with over the years has been shocked and almost depressed when they first hear the recorded calls made by their phone people (call center). However, once you begin to measure what you treasure, create a culture of accountability, and you commit to providing on-going training, your "call people" will improve. I would challenge you here and now to write out the answers to the following questions for your betterment:

 What call recording system do you currently use to record your phone calls? *Email info@thrive15.com for recommended call recording systems.

_____

 On a scale of 1 to 10 (with 10 being the highest), how confident are you that your team is following your systems and processes on each and every call?

_____

 How much do you believe it may be costing you to have your team performing poorly when answering your phones on your behalf?

_____

MOVE #21

SET UP GPS ON THE CARS OF YOUR
EMPLOYEES.

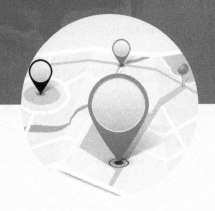

NOTABLE QUOTABLE

"Trust, but verify."

- PRESIDENT RONALD REAGAN

(President Ronald Reagan was the 40th President of the United States from 1981 to 1989. Before he became president he was the 33rd Governor of California, from 1967 to 1975. Prior to entering the world of politics he was a Hollywood actor. He is a man who knew how to get things done.)

From my experience, if you have people that work for you and you are paying for their gas, 7 out of 10 of them are going to take advantage of you and lie about their mileage. If you do not put a GPS device on their vehicles to monitor the actual distances, they will take the company car out for sushi, out to a movie, and on an extended road trip. You must watch them like a hawk (assuming that hawks monitor their miles intensely). When you start to intensely analyze the mileage turned in by your team members, you will quickly discover that they "magically" become more productive. I would challenge you here and now to write out the answers to the following questions for your betterment:

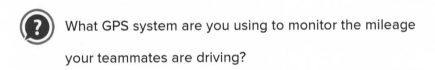 What GPS system are you using to monitor the mileage your teammates are driving?

_____

How many miles / hours per year do you estimate that your team is currently wasting as a result of you not measuring their miles via a transparent GPS monitoring system?

_____

MOVE #22

SETUP RECORDED VIDEOS IN YOUR OFFICES, WORKSHOPS, AND ASSEMBLY LINES.

FUN FACT

"The U.S. Chamber of Commerce estimates that 75%

of employees steal from the workplace and that most

do so repeatedly."

- Employee Theft: Are You Blind to It?

- CBS News - Money Watch

Oh, it's amazing how productivity in your business improves when you decide to "trust but verify" everything via video cameras. The "jack-assery" that is caught within every organization is amazing. The lies, the cheating, the stealing, and lateness are all exposed immediately and you get to analyze what's really hurting your business. My friend, if you sincerely care about getting more stuff and getting your people to get more stuff done, you simply have to install video cameras in your offices, workshops, assembly lines, gyms, retail stores, etc. I would challenge you here and now to write out the answers to the following questions for your betterment:

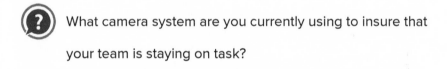 What camera system are you currently using to insure that your team is staying on task?

_____

How many hours do you estimate that your team is losing per day due to unproductivity and not being held accountable via video recordings?

_____

How much money do you estimate that it's costing you (in poor employee performance) to not have video cameras installed in your place of business?

_____

MOVE #23

REMOVE ALL INTERACTION (WHEN POSSIBLE) WITH PEOPLE THAT DO NOT SHARE YOUR VISION, YOUR VALUES AND WORK ETHIC.

NOTABLE QUOTABLE

"Most people think it's all about ideas--It's not. doing the work &
turning your ideas into reality."

- CLAY CLARK

In public school, you had to sit next to people because of the zip code their family chose to live in. However, in real life you don't have to hang out with people simply because you live near them. In fact, I would encourage you to avoid interactions with people that do not share your values or work ethic because you will find yourselves becoming chronically agitated with each other. As an example, I sincerely do not care about fishing or camping. In fact, if almost anybody on the planet asked me to go camping, I would say "no" because I sincerely dislike it.

Thus, I don't invest any of my time with Boy Scouts, Royal Rangers, and other organizations who have a love for camping. I don't understand lazy people who refuse to put in the work it takes to grow a successful business. I don't invest time with people who chronically sleep in and who view working hard as something to be avoided. Why? I don't want to spend my day unproductively arguing with people that don't share my values or my work ethic and you shouldn't either.

I would challenge you here and now to write out the answers to the following questions for your betterment:

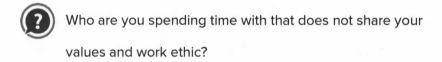 Who are you spending time with that does not share your values and work ethic?

_____

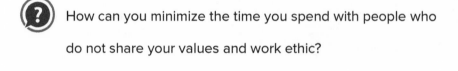 How can you minimize the time you spend with people who do not share your values and work ethic?

_____

MOVE #24

STOP EMOTIONALLY
ENGAGING WITH SOCIAL MEDIA
COMMENTS AND REVIEWS ABOUT YOU
AND YOUR BUSINESS.

NOTABLE QUOTABLE

"The fastest way to change yourself is to hang out with people

who are already the way you want to be."

- REID HOFFMAN

(Reid is the founder of LinkedIn, and he's a successful venture capitalist and author. He's currently a partner at the venture capital firm Greylock Partners. On the Forbes 2017 list of the world's billionaires, Hoffman was ranked #631 with a net worth of $3.1 billion. He knows how to get things done.)

I really do care about the businesses that I have built because they provide for my family (DJConnection.com, EpicPhotos.com, EITRLounge.com, ThriveTimeShow.com, MakeYourLifeEpic.com, PartyProRents.com, etc.). On the other hand, I do not care about the endless negativity posted about me and our businesses on social media. As an example, at Elephant In The Room, we employ a team of almost 100 people who sincerely do their very best job to cut your hair at the highest quality standard in the business. However, we currently have decided to have humans cut your hair and not robots. Thus, approximately 1 out of 34 times, people are going to mess up, and somebody is going to get upset every 34 haircuts because a human is cutting their hair.

Fortunately, most people understand that mistakes happen, yet some idiots cannot grasp this idea. They will invest the majority of an evening on social media trying to destroy our company or myself personally.

If I sincerely valued the comments posted about me and our team, I would end up losing my mind.

I would challenge you here and now to write out the answers to the following questions for your betterment:

 In what ways do you need to stop emotionally engaging with social media comments?

_____

 In what ways to do you need to stop emotionally engaging with reviews, critics and negative feedback from people who do not have a valid opinion?

_____

MOVE #25

TAKE A 5 MINUTE TIME-OUT BEFORE
RESPONDING TO ANYTHING SERIOUS
IN YOUR LIFE.

NOTABLE QUOTABLE

"I like work/life separation, not work/life balance. What I mean by that is, if I'm on, I want to be on and maximally productive. If I'm off, I don't want to think about work. When people strive for work/life balance, they end up blending them. That's how you end up checking

email all day Saturday."

- TIM FERRISS

(Tim has written many self-help books on the "4-hour" theme, some of the books he's written have been featured in the New York Times, Wall Street Journal, and the USA Today bestseller lists, starting with The 4-Hour Workweek. Tim has been an angel investor and an advisor to Facebook, Twitter, Evernote, and Uber, and many other companies. He's a man who gets things done.)

During our lives, both you and I could make an insanely long list of the bad things that people have done to us, but if we did that we would become very negative people. My friends, my recommendation is that you recognize the *Bible* as correct when it states in Deuteronomy 32:35, "It is mine to avenge; I will repay. In due time their foot will slip, their day of disaster is near and their doom rushes upon them."

In fact, in Romans 12:19 the Bible also states, "Do not take revenge, my dear friends, but leave room for God's wrath, for it is written, 'It is mine to avenge; I will repay,' says the Lord."

My point is this, don't waste your time freaking out the moment something terrible happens. In fact, take a minimum of 5 minutes and 100 deep breaths before you respond to something terrible that somebody has said about you, your team, or your wife. I would even suggest taking a whole 24 hours before responding.

I would challenge you here and now to write out the answers to the following questions for your betterment:

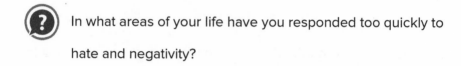 In what areas of your life have you responded too quickly to hate and negativity?

_____

What are current areas of your life where you are fanning the flames of hate and wasting massive amounts of time because you are responding instantly to the grievances, and the issues of the day?

_____

MOVE #26

DON'T ALLOW YOURSELF TO BE
GUILTED INTO DOING THINGS THAT YOU
DON'T WANT TO DO.

Just because someone invites you to a party does not mean that they have earned the right to put something on your schedule. Once you have kids in school, you will see what I'm talking about. If your kid is in a class with 24 classmates and they are in a gymnastics class with 18 other kids that is a total of 42 total kids whose birthday parties you may be invited to by default. In my case, we have 5 kids, 2 grandmas, 1 grandpa, one brother, and two brother-in-laws that all have birthdays. If we took time out of our schedule to celebrate a birthday with all 50 of these people, we would be blocking off at least ONE DAY EVERY WEEK to celebrate and I couldn't then find the time to host a daily live radio show.

....

1. Buy Billy a birthday card.

2. Buy Billy a gift card.

3. Write something thoughtful in the newsletter

4. Hire a babysitter so that we can attend Billy's birthday party.

5. Call Billy to confirm that we are going to attend his birthday party.

6. Find Billy on Facebook and write a birthday well wish for him.

I would challenge you here and now to write out the answers

to the following questions for your betterment:

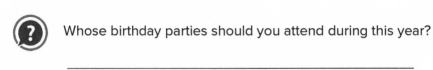 Whose birthday parties should you attend during this year?

_____

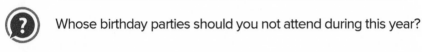 Whose birthday parties should you not attend during this year?

_____

How many hours did you waste during this past year

attending birthday parties for kids, coworkers, fellow

church members and people that you don't really know and

that your kids don't even really know?

_____

MOVE #27

STOP BUYING THINGS YOU
DON'T NEED.

NOTABLE QUOTABLE

"Financial peace isn't the acquisition of stuff. It's learning to live on less than you make, so you can give money back and have money to invest. You can't win until you do this."

- DAVE RAMSEY

(The famous author, radio host, and speaker, television personality, and motivational speaker who has helped thousands of people to become debt free. He's also a man known for getting stuff done.)

Anytime you buy something, you have also bought the responsibility to maintain and insure it. If you want to get more stuff done you must learn to stop acquiring things that you don't need, or you will fill your schedule up with the endless maintenance needs of material items (like your boat, your lake house, your garden, your greenhouse, your dogs, etc.) I would challenge you, here and now, to write out the answers to the following questions for your betterment:

? What items did you buy during the past 2 years that you regret purchasing?

_____

? What are items that you could rent for enjoyment rather than buy (boats, exotic cars, ec.)?

_____

? What are items that you could sell or get rid of that are costing you both time and money to maintain that you rarely use?

_____

MOVE #28

COMMIT TO SIMPLICITY.

NOTABLE QUOTABLES

"Brevity is the soul of wit."

- WILLIAM SHAKESPEARE

(The most well known playwright and actor, in the history of the English language and the world's pre-eminent dramatist.)

"That's been one of my mantras - focus and simplicity. Simple can be harder than complex: You have to work hard to get your thinking clean to make it simple. But it's worth it in the end because once you get there, you can move mountains."

- STEVE JOBS

(The man who personally lead the charge to make personal computers that non-nerds could use, the man who co-founded Apple, the man who introduced the first 100% digitally animated box office success story (Toy Story) when he was the CEO of the company. The man who revolutionized the music industry the iPod and iTunes. The man who introduced the iPad tablet technology to the planet and the man who introduced the game-changing phone, the iPhone to the planet. He was a dude who got things done.)

NOTABLE QUOTABLES

"Truth is ever to be found in simplicity, and not in the multiplicity and confusion of things."

- ISAAC NEWTON

(The English mathematician, astronomer, and physicist known as the most influential scientist of all time.)

"Almost all quality improvement comes via simplification of design, manufacturing, layout, processes, and procedures."

- TOM PETERS

(The bestselling author of In Search of Excellence (co-authored with Robert H. Waterman, Jr.)

NOTABLE QUOTABLE

"If you can't explain it to a six year old, you don't understand it yourself."

- ALBERT EINSTEIN

(The famous German-born theoretical physicist who developed the theory of relativity, and who convinced president Franklin Delano Roosevelt to fund the development of the atomic bombs we dropped to end World War II.)

The more time that you invest to study the minds of the greats, Steve Jobs, William Shakespeare, etc., you will discover that simplicity truly is the ultimate sophistication. Neither you or I want to be greeted with a massive task list each morning and we don't want to have to employ a team of geniuses to simply make our at-home-technology work because we can't figure it out. Keep it simple and you will get more stuff done. I would challenge you here and now to write out the answers to the following questions for your betterment:

? In what ways can you simplify your business processes?

_____

_____

? In what ways can you simplify your life?

_____

_____

? In what ways can you simplify your daily schedule?

_____

_____

MOVE #29

AVOID THE PHYSICAL AND EMOTIONAL
PRESENCE OF CHRONICALLY LATE AND
EMOTIONAL PEOPLE
(WHEN POSSIBLE).

NOTABLE QUOTABLE

"You will not have a positive life if you spend your time with negative and dramatic people."

- CLAY CLARK

We all have choices to make - do we want to be early, on-time, or late? Do we want to bring joy, laughter and charm to every conversation or do we want to "keep it real," negative and depressing? People who choose to bring hate and negativity to every conversation must not have a consistent daily presence in your life or you will become a negative person over time by default. I would challenge you here and now to write out the answers to the following questions for your betterment:

 Who in your life is consistently negative?

_____

 What can you do to reduce the amount of interactivity that you spend with this chronically negative person on a daily basis?

_____

 Who in your life is consistently late?

_____

 What can you do to minimize the amount of time that you spend with chronically late people in your life?

_____

MOVE #30

TURN PUSH NOTIFICATIONS OFF ON
YOUR COMPUTER, YOUR PHONE AND
ON EVERY DIGITAL DEVICE.

NOTABLE QUOTABLE

"I think that modern world is actually really bad. The modern world is full of distractions. Things like Twitter and Facebook are not making you happy. They are making you unhappy. You are essentially playing a game that's created by the creators of those systems, and yes, it can be a useful game once in a blue moon. You are engaging in the dispute, and resentment, comparison, jealousy, anger about things that frankly just don't matter."

- NAVAL RAVIKANT

(Naval Ravikant is the CEO and a co-founder of the online fund resource for entrepreneurs called AngelList. He previously co-founded Epinions (which went public as part of Shopping.com) and Vast.com. He's still a very active Angel investor, and has chosen to invest in dozens of companies, including Twitter, Uber, Yammer, Stack Overflow and Wanelo.)

As a rule, I try to minimize the amount of time that I spend on social media during my day between zero and 10 minutes. Yet for the sake of this book, I am hopping onto Facebook to give you real-time data and real-life feedback about how I could be wasting my time if only I were more committed to "The Facebook Life."

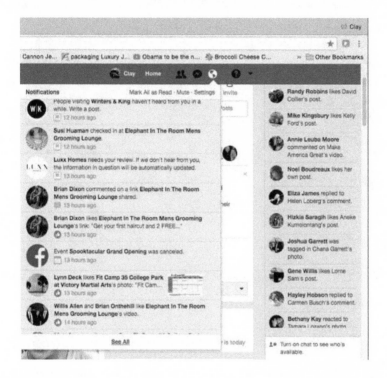

Essentially it looks like I missed out on Hayley's comments to Carmen, Gene liking Sam, Bethany reacting to Lozann's photo, Eliza commenting to Helen, Lynn liking Fit Camp, 1 person being frustrated with one of my companies, Susi checking in, Spooktacular canceling their grand opening, a company that needs my review and a general

THE ART OF GETTING THINGS DONE

buffet of "who-gives-a-crap." It was exhausting even listing out all the notifications that I "missed out on." Now let's see what I'm missing out on by not responding to my Facebook messages (God forbid if we did this on Linkedin, Youtube, and Twitter.

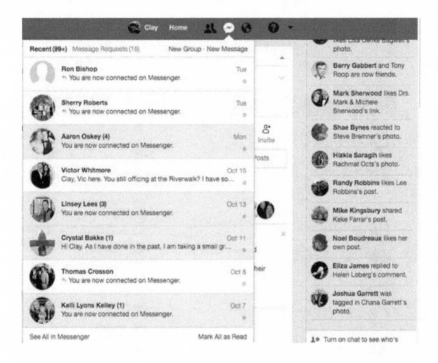

So it looks like I'm connected on messenger to many new people and that someone who once screwed me over repeatedly in business deals is now trying to, yet again, reach out to me. If I checked my social media updates every month, let alone every day, I wouldn't get anything done. Now, if I totally wanted to become less efficient and to waste massive amounts of time, I need to go back and add these notifications back onto my smartphone.

172

I would challenge you here and now to write out the answers to the following questions for your betterment:

? How many hours per week to you devote to social media?

_____

? How many times do you allow social media to interrupt your concentration, conversation, vocation, or vacation during a typical day?

_____

? How often do you let negative social media comments and posts impact your present emotional state?

_____

? Who should you unfriend on social media today?

_____

? Who should you unfriend in "real life" too?

_____

MOVE #31

BLOCK NEGATIVE PEOPLE AND
RELATIONSHIPS THAT YOU NEED TO
BREAK TIES WITH FROM YOUR PHONE,
YOUR EMAIL AND YOUR
SOCIAL MEDIA.

NOTABLE QUOTABLE

"I used to sip the whiskey and hit the bong. I gave that up, now all my friends are gone. And my folks don't understand I ain't no macho man. But I know how to write one hell of a song."

- MIKE POSNER

(Mike Posner began his career as a record producer, creating music with his friend Big Sean. Posner produced and was featured on Big Sean's first mixtape and on the song, titled "Smoke & Drive." Mike's second mixtape, A Matter of Time started getting attention from the music industry in 2009. Mike worked with Don Cannon and DJ Benzi to create the mixtape which was released through Small Town Records while he was at Duke University under the name, "Mike Posner & the Brain Trust." The Brain Trust was in reference to Mike's supporters. The release was odd in that it was shared for free through iTunes, a channel designed for educational audio content only. Although he wasn't the only musician to expose this loophole, the record release gained a great response. Immediately his songs hit the number one position on the iTunes chart. Posner then got a record deal with J Records (RCA/Sony) in July 2009, after completing his Junior year at Duke University. On April 15, 2015, Posner released the acoustic song, "I Took a Pill in Ibiza", on his YouTube account. This song was shared via an album called The Truth that Mike shared for free with his fans through his email list. Mike later announced that his album would be available for purchase on June 22. In addition, Posner then announced that his second studio album was going to be released after. "I Took a Pill in Ibiza" was then remixed by the Norwegian producer duo, SeeB. The version of this song gained nearly 750 million streams on Spotify and hit number two on the Global Top 50 Chart and reached number five on the USA Top 50 Chart. Throughout his career he has both written and produced hit songs for Justin Bieber, Labrynth, Maroon 5, Snoop Dog, Big Sean, and other top artists.)

In my endless quest to help you achieve your F6 goals, (faith, family, friendship, fitness, finances, fun goals) I would encourage you to block out the negative people and relationships that you have in your life. Block them from your phone, your email, and your social media, it's amazingly freeing. I love not knowing what the hundreds of people I have fired are doing. I love not knowing what college campuses are protesting. I love not being sent GoFundMe requests from lazy-ass people I've fired. I love not receiving real time email updates about how life is terrible from family members. I would challenge you here and now to write out the answers to the following questions for your betterment:

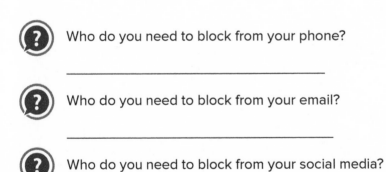

Who do you need to block from your phone?

_____

Who do you need to block from your email?

_____

Who do you need to block from your social media?

_____

Who do you need to block from your text messages?

_____

MOVE #32

SAY HELLO TO THE PERSON WHO
INVITED YOU TO PARTY AND THEN
LEAVE AS SOON AS POSSIBLE.

NOTABLE QUOTABLE

"Your time is limited, so don't waste it living someone else's life. Don't be trapped by dogma - which is living with the results of other people's thinking. Don't let the noise of others' opinions drown out your own inner voice. And most important, have the courage to follow your heart and intuition."

- STEVE JOBS

(A man who was able to change the world in part because he was unbelievably effective at blocking out all distractions that got in the way of his work and focus. He was a dude who got things done.)

When I first started DJConnection.com, I was sincerely excited and honored to be invited to any event. If you invited me to a Chamber event, a Grand Opening celebration, a Ribbon Cutting, or any kind of function I was honored and excited to attend. Then I realized that I was spending nearly every free evening we had with random people while claiming that I did not have enough time to make progress towards the achievement of my goals. But now, I have a move.

When I'm invited to an event that I must attend out of obligation, I make sure to say hello to the person who invited me as soon as possible so that they know I attended. Then as soon as they get engaged in conversations with other attendees, I leave. Typically, they don't even recognize that I left. I would challenge you here and now to write out the answers to the following questions for your betterment:

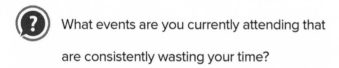 What events are you currently attending that are consistently wasting your time?

_____

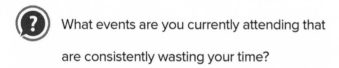 What is the next big obligation event that you can try out this super move on?

_____

MOVE #33

WAKE UP 2 HOURS BEFORE MOST
PEOPLE DO AND GO TO BED 2 HOURS
BEFORE MOST PEOPLE DO.

NOTABLE QUOTABLE

"Early to bed and early to rise makes a man healthy,
wealthy, and wise."

- BENJAMIN FRANKLIN

*(The main author of the United States Constitution and the man responsible
for securing the support from the French needed to beat the British during the
Revolutionary War.)*

It's mind blowing how much you can get done before most people even wake up. As an example, I have completely written this manuscript between the hours of 3 AM and 9 AM. I sketched out the book outlines during the day, but I have knocked out writing the entire book when most people are still sound asleep. When you are uninterrupted, you will find yourself flying through your to-do list. You will knock out items in minutes that would typically require hours of your time if you attempted them amidst the constant distractions of the day.

I would challenge you here and now to become proactive about designing your life one day at a time by getting up and going to bed 2 hours before everyone else. This week, during this early meta time, I have taken time to do all of the following items and more:

- ✔ *Schedule one of my daughter's birthdays (we have 4)*
- ✔ *Design a berm building (a building built into the land) for our new office location*
- ✔ *Write down the list of reasons why I am going to fire somebody today who has been secretly doing nefarious and business damaging activities during the past 2 months, but who has worked with us for about 4 years.*
- ✔ *Plan out the right time to go and get my driver's license. (However, there is never really a good time to go to the tag agency unless you are doing research for a book on how not to do customer service.)*
- ✔ *Plan out his week's radio show broadcasts.*
- ✔ *Write out the lyrics to a new song that I am working on.*

My friend, I encourage you to write out the answers to the following questions for your betterment:

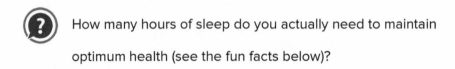 How many hours of sleep do you actually need to maintain optimum health (see the fun facts below)?

_____

 What time can you commit to waking up every morning?

_____

FUN FACT

The Mayo Clinic recommends that adults should get between 7 to 9 hours of sleep per day. How many hours of sleep are good enough for good health?

MOVE #34

WEAR THE SAME THING
EVERYDAY.

Whether you analyze the life and times of President Barack Obama, Mark Zuckerberg, Dr. Dre, or Steve Jobs, you will start to discover that many of the world's most effective people wear the same thing every day. For years I wore a blue suit, a white shirt, and a red tie because it minimized decisions and freed up my mind and the time I needed to knock out other more productive things. Now I wear a ThriveTime Show Business Coach Radio Show hoodie, a hat with the word "BOOM" or the ThriveTimeShow.com logo on it, white Adidas shoes, blue jeans and a black $5 t-shirt I bought from Wal-Mart. When I'm working out, I wear And1 basketball shorts that I bought from Wal-Mart for $9.97.

I would challenge you here and now to write out the answers to the following questions for your betterment:

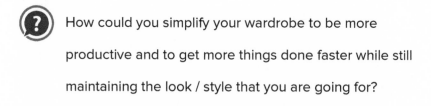 How could you simplify your wardrobe to be more productive and to get more things done faster while still maintaining the look / style that you are going for?

_____

When is the first week that you would be willing to wear the same thing for an entire week just to see what happens?

_____

MOVE #35

AUTOMATE YOUR SAVINGS WITH A
ONE-TIME DECISION TO SAVE.

NOTABLE QUOTABLE

"In fact, what determines your wealth is not how much you make but how much you keep of what you make."

- DAVID BACH

(The best-selling author of The Automatic Millionaire.)

When you take the time to make the one-time decision to automate your savings, you will reap a lifetime of riches and financial freedom as a result. My friend, the power of compound interest is magic when you have it working for you and your savings, but you have to make the one-time decision to actually set aside and save a specific percentage of your gross earnings. I highly recommend that you would save a minimum of 5% of your gross income. When you implement the proven business growth strategies, you will earn a lot more money, but that won't matter if you don't save anything. It's not about how much money you earn, it's about how much money you keep.

I have essentially been self-employed since the age of 16 (21 years as of the writing of this book), and I have always been able to earn as much money as I want. It is possible to have financial freedom while being your own boss. Maybe you already have been able to generate copious amounts of cash. If not, I know that when you implement the strategies that we teach in the Start Here: The World's Best Business Growth and Consulting Book: Business Growth Strategies from the World's Best Business Coach, you will earn a ton of gross revenue, but none of that matters if you don't save anything.

I would challenge you here and now to write out the answers to the following questions for your betterment:

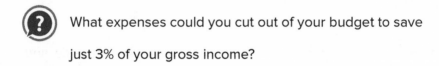 What expenses could you cut out of your budget to save just 3% of your gross income?

_____

When will you meet with your financial advisors to begin finding an investment vehicle that is safe and that you can trust (specific date and time)?

_____

Who will you meet with to help you plan your financial future?

_____

NOTABLE QUOTABLES

"Compound interest is the eighth wonder of the world. He who understands it, earns it ... he who doesn't ... pays it."

- ALBERT EINSTEIN

*(The famous physicist who was obsessed with
the power of compound interest.)*

"You need to have a proactive approach to managing your
personal finances and your accounting. Your accounting needs
to be viewed as a front dashboard and not just a rear view
mirror. Decide one time to automate the amount of money that you
want to save as a percentage of your income and you will
become wealthy over time as a result."

- PAUL HOOD, CPA

(The founder of HoodCPAs.com)

MOVE #36

AVOID DISCUSSIONS ABOUT OPINIONS
AND FEELINGS...YOU WANT TO FOCUS
ON FACTS.

NOTABLE QUOTABLE

"A pessimist sees the difficulty in every opportunity; an optimist sees the opportunity in every difficulty."

- WINSTON CHURCHILL

(The Prime Minister of the United Kingdom from 1940 to 1945 and again from 1951 to 1955. Who stood up and fought against the Nazi regime long before the United States pledged our support. He was defiant despite the certain doom his people faced as a result of his decision to not turn over his Jewish citizens to the Nazis.)

I get a lot done during my day because 95% of my discussions are about finding proactive case-study proven solutions to existing known problems based upon facts and not feelings. If I wanted to dramatically slow down my rate of success, I would begin investing massive amounts of time talking about my feelings and the feelings of our team.

Because the emotions and feelings of most people are constantly changing, most conversations would never end. In fact, I could invest thousands upon thousands of hours arguing with somebody about the certain mediocrity in our school systems that was created as a result of offering America's public school teachers tenure (in fact I probably just irritated you or someone you know). If you want to get stuff done, you need to avoid talking to people about their feelings unless you are married to them and want to continue having sex with them (in the context of marriage of course).

I would challenge you here and now to write out the answers to the following questions for your betterment:

What conversations did you waste time on this week discussing feelings during your workday?

_____

What feelings high-drama focused people do you need to try to spend less time talking with during your work day?

_____

What accusations made against you by Obama voters who can't stop getting divorced and vaping do you need to ignore?

_____

MOVE #37

IF YOU HAVE TO MEET, MEET FOR
COFFEE AND NOT LUNCH.

NOTABLE QUOTABLE

"Remember that time is money."

- BENJAMIN FRANKLIN

(A man who seems to have achieved 50 times more in his lifetime than most people achieve in their lifetime.)

....

I used to agree to meet people for lunch during my work day all of the time. I found myself meeting with my attorney for lunch, a potential vendor for lunch, and the "Yellow Page Advertising Guy" for lunch (yes that used to be a thing). Then it occurred to me, what if I just started meeting these people at my office or for coffee?

As I grew my wealth, I became more intense about never leaving my office. Now I almost never leave my office at all during the work-day which is why I am so pale and so deficient in Vitamin D.

I would challenge you here and now to write out the answers to the following questions for your betterment:

? What lunch meetings could you stop going to starting now or sooner?

_____

? What people could you start meeting for coffee and not lunch?

_____

? How many minutes have you invested this year to driving to lunch and coffee?

_____

? What people could you start meeting at your office and only your office?

_____

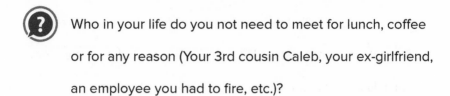

Who in your life do you not need to meet for lunch, coffee or for any reason (Your 3rd cousin Caleb, your ex-girlfriend, an employee you had to fire, etc.)?

_____

When will you ship me some vitamin D to make up for my skins lack of access to direct sunlight?

_____

MOVE #38

WORK VIA APPOINTMENT ONLY,
DO NOT EVER PARTICIPATE IN
THE TIME WASTING GAME
OF "PHONE TAG."

NOTABLE QUOTABLE

"You've got to know what you want. This is central to acting on your intentions. When you know what you want, you realize that all there is left then is time management. You'll manage your time to achieve your goals because you clearly know what you're trying to achieve in your life."

- PATCH ADAMS

(The 1998 major motion picture Patch Adams was based on Patch's life and times. Patch Adams also did not like the film and said of Robin Williams in an interview, "He made $21 million for four months of pretending to be me, in a very simplistic version, and did not give $10 to my free hospital. Patch Adams, the person, would have, if I had Robin's money, given all $21 million to a free hospital in a country where 80 million cannot get care.)

You must end every sales call and every management related call with the question, "When do you want me to follow-up with you?" You must be very specific about the time that you are going to call them, the day, and the time zone that they are in. If you don't do these things, you will be playing the soul-sucking and time wasting game called, "Phone Tag." I would challenge you here and now to write out the answers to the following questions for your betterment:

 When will you begin working via appointment only and stop playing the soul-sucking and time-wasting game of phone tag?

_____

 What is a project that you have allowed to drift as a result of playing phone tag?

_____

MOVE #39

QUIT YOUR TIME-
CONSUMING BAD HABITS.

NOTABLE QUOTABLE

"I don't think modern science has good answers here. I think that modern world is actually really bad. The modern world is full of distractions. Things like Twitter and Facebook are not making you happy. They are making you unhappy. You are essentially playing a game that's created by the creators of those systems, and yes, it can be a useful game once in a blue moon. You are engaging in the dispute, and resentment, comparison, jealousy, anger about things that frankly just don't matter."

- NAVAL RAVIKANT

(A man who has invested in social media companies because of their addictive nature but who thinks on a personal level none of US should be using it. He's invested in many successful companies including Twitter, Uber, Yammer, Stack Overflow and Wanelo.)

As a business coach, I am routinely asked by entrepreneurs to help them to enhance their personal productivity and the overall productivity and time management skills of their entire team.

However, before I ever begin suggesting specific schedule enhancements and game-changing new approaches to feedback loops, quality control systems, and workflow enhancements I simply ask everyone to log what they did yesterday and what they are doing today.

AMPLE EXAMPLE:

8:00 AM - Arrived at work

9:00 AM - Made sales call with Karl Smith

9:10 AM - Closed the deal with the Rogers Account

9:40 AM - Service work

11:30 AM - Left to go to lunch

12:30 PM - Returned from lunch

It's amazing what we discover when people actually invest the time to log what they are specifically doing during their work day. People cannot seem to explain where their time went.

They seem to be unable to list out what they did during vast portions of their day. The day did in fact happen and they were physically present at work. So what happened during their day and where did all of their time go? My friend, sadly, here is where most of the time went.

The 10 Most Common time wasting activities people engage in at work:

1. Social Media Interaction

2. Mental Drifting

3. Alcohol

4. Drugs

5. New Girlfriend Chasing

6. Looking at Adult Content During the Work Day

7. Non-Work Related Email

8. Over-Spiritualizing Everything

9. Engaging in Lingering Arguments

10. Emotionally Lamenting Over Everything

FUN FACT

"The 2014 data is in from Salary.com, who gathered the responses of 750 employees. Their verdict: the challenge of wasted workplace time is even worse than before. A year ago, 69% of respondents said they waste at least some time at work on a daily basis. But the number of people who now admit to wasting time at work every day has reached a whopping 89%."

- Wasting Time at Work: The Epidemic Continues

- Cheryl Conner - Forbes

NOTABLE QUOTABLE

"I believe that the secret of your success is determined by your daily agenda. If you make a few key decisions and then manage them well in your daily agenda, you will succeed. You will never change your life until you change something you do daily."

- JOHN MAXWELL

(The former pastor turned best-selling author of The 21 Irrefutable Laws of Leadership and The 21 Indispensable Qualities of a Leader.)

I would challenge you here and now to write out the answers to the following question for your betterment:

1. What did you do yesterday (go ahead and list it out) on the lines below:

_____

_____

_____

_____

_____

_____

_____

_____

_____

_____

_____

_____

_____

_____

MOVE #40

QUIT INTERVIEWING
CANDIDATES
ONE PERSON AT A TIME.

FUN FACT: According to research conducted by the U.S. Chamber of Commerce in conjunction with CBS News and The Money Watch program, "The U.S. Chamber of Commerce estimates that 75% of employees steal from the workplace and that most do so repeatedly." https://www.cbsnews.com/news/employee-theft-are-you-blind-to-it/

Did your parents ever teach you that a quitter never wins and that a winner never quits? Their parents never did.

 FUN FACT: Despite being in a deep economic recession at the time, a July 7th, 2010 article published by the Harvard Business Review reported that more employees quit their jobs than were terminated, according to the US Bureau of Labor. Do you remember when college was supposed to make you more intelligent and more hirable? They don't.

 FUN FACT: According to a USA Today Article written by Mary Beth Marklein, research shows students spent 50% less time studying compared with students a few decades ago. The research compared college students enrolled in 2001 versus college students enrolled in 2011.

Do you remember when it wasn't normal for people to look at adult content during their workday (or other parts of their day)?

FUN FACT: "70 percent of all online porn access occurs during the nine-to-five workday." (Porn at Work: Recognizing a Sex Addict, - Gloria McDonald, CNBC) Whatever happened to common sense?

FUN FACT: In a 2011 Newsweek Article, research was conducted by asking 1,000 U.S. citizens to take America's official citizenship test. Twenty nine percent (29%) couldn't name the Vice President.

FUN FACT: According to Gail Cunningham, spokeswoman for the National Foundation of Credit Counseling, as quoted in a July 2012 article in Newsweek Magazine, 56% of U.S. adults admit they don't have a budget; one-third don't pay all their bills on time.

FUN FACT: According to an article written by Mary Beth Marklein in *USA Today*. Nearly half of the nation's undergraduates show almost no gains in learning (in their testing or critical thinking skills) in their first two years of college. The report concludes this is because, in large part, colleges don't make academics a priority. Among their top activities, students report spending 24% of their time sleeping, 51% of their time socializing and just 7% actually studying.

FUN FACT: In a study published in Inc. Magazine in June of 2007 and written by Liz Webber, research showed that average employees wasted an average of 1.7 hours of an 8.5 hour workday, while 20-29 year olds wasting 2.1 hours per day.

FUN FACT: A Leadership IQ study of 6,000 workers featured on Fox News in 2008 revealed that in 2008 nearly 25% of the average American's workday was wasted. Thus, the average employee was reported to waste nearly 2.3 hours per day.

FUN FACT: In a February 22, 2010 article featured in Inc. Magazine and written by Kim Boatman research conducted by SpectorSoft Corp, concluded that 89% of the businesses that were studied discovered employees were wasting time or abusing Internet use.

 FUN FACT: According to research conducted by Research Basex and reported in a February issue of USA Today "productivity losses due to the cost of unnecessary interruptions" were at $650 billion in 2007.

 FUN FACT: In a 2002 article published by NY Times Best-Selling Author Ken Blanchard, a large survey of 1,300 private-sector companies, conducted by Proudfoot Consulting, found that on average only 59% of work time is productive.

 FUN FACT: A March 2, 2011 study published by Inc. Magazine reports that employees are unproductive for half of the day. In an article posted by Martha C. White on March 13th, 2012 entitled, "*You're Wasting Time at Work Right Now, Aren't You?*" revealed that a 2012 study of 3,200 employees conducted by Salary.com showed that 64% say they visit websites unrelated to work daily. Do you remember when 1 out of 5 of your co-workers wasn't insane? They don't.

FUN FACT: According to a disturbing article published by Harvard Health Publications in February of 2010, researchers analyzing results from the U.S. National Comorbidity Survey found a nationally representative study of Americans ages 15 to 54. In that study it was reported that 18% of those who were employed said they experienced symptoms of a mental health disorder in the previous month.

Don't over-think this concept, just implement the following action steps and you will win:

1. Write a great job post (if you don't know how to do this subscribe at ThriveTimeShow.com and you will gain access to our proven templates.)
2. Post your job posts every week on Craigslist.com, Indeed.com and on your business Facebook account.
3. Respond to all job applicants inviting them to interview with you (don't read their resumes and don't tell them it is a group interview format).
4. Disqualify anybody who shows up late to the job interview.
5. Disqualify anybody who looks like, smells like or sounds like they are currently a drug addict.

6. Disqualify anybody who argues with you during the interview.

7. Have the most likable candidate shadow you for a 1-2 hours (a 1/2 day maximum) day of work.

8. If you like them after they have shadowed you, read their resume and do a background check.

9. Offer them a job.

10. Train them on a daily basis. Commit to being a source of wisdom for them. Inspire them. Recognize that management today is about mentorship.

Most employees today come from broken homes where they were raised by idiots, addicts or absent parents and it is not their fault. Today's employees just need to be coached up, mentored and loved on and they will succeed.

Note: To learn every single aspect of the entire "Group Interview" process, book your tickets to our next interactive 15-hour 2-day ThriveTime Show business conference by buying your tickets at ThriveTimeShow.com today.

I would challenge you here and now to write out the answers to the following question for your betterment:

 How much time have you wasted this year doing job interviews with candidates who did not even show up on time to the actual first interview?

_____

 With your current hiring process, how long will it take you to actually find the high-quality people that you are searching for?

_____

 Why are most people (not you) completely opposed to doing a group interview as opposed to doing one-on-one interviews?

_____

MOVE #41

DON'T RESPOND TO MOST EMAIL,
SOCIAL MEDIA POSTS, TEXT MESSAGES
AND PHONE CALLS.

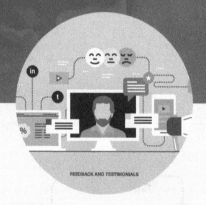

FEEDBACK AND TESTIMONIALS

NOTABLE QUOTABLE

"When you carry a digital gadget that creates a virtual link to the office, you need to create a virtual boundary that didn't exist before."

- DANIEL GOLEMAN

(A psychologist, Ph.D., and the best-selling author of the New York Times bestseller Emotional Intelligence and Social Intelligence: The New Science of Human Relationships. For twelve years, he also wrote articles for the The New York Times. He focuses on writing about behavioral sciences.)

WE NEED TO RE-CREATE BOUNDARIES.

Today anybody who can correctly guess your email address has access to you if you made the poor decision to sync your email address to your smartphone. In fact, there are programs that exist that will actually scan websites and provide you with a list of emails within seconds.

We live in such a crazy time now that anyone on the planet who wants to get a hold of you can. People can instantly get access to you if you made the mistake of syncing your smartphone to your social media accounts. My friend, giving just anyone the ability to gain instant access to you is not good for your work performance, your mental health, or your soul.

While I've been writing this manuscript, I am sure that I have missed numerous, and potentially countless attempts by low quality, mid-quality and high-quality humans who are trying to reach me. But for the sake of this exercise, I'm going to pause for a brief moment to actually count how many exciting potential interruptions I might be missing out on today...I'll be right back...(It's 3:21 AM)

AND THE TOTALS AS OF 3:29 AM ARE

- Missed Calls - 7 (Today, thus far)
- Missed Facebook Friend Requests - 2 (Today, thus far)
- Missed Facebook Messages - 6 (Today, thus far)
- Missed Facebook Notifications - 27 (Today, thus far)
- Linkedin My Network Notifications - 57 (Today, thus far)
- Linkedin Messages - 2 (Today, thus far)
- Linkedin Notifications - 41 (Today, thus far)
- Voice Messages - 2 (Today, thus far)
- Text Messages - 14 (Today, thus far)
- Youtube Notifications - 37 (Today, thus far)
- Twitter Notifications - 31 (Today, thus far)
- Total Potential Interruptions = 226 (And it's only 3:33 AM)

I would challenge you here and now to write out the answers to the following questions for your betterment:

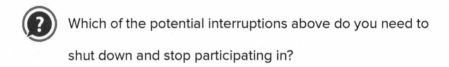 Which of the potential interruptions above do you need to shut down and stop participating in?

_____

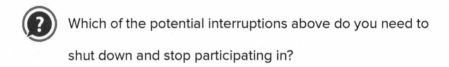 How many times during your typical day do you allow yourself to be interrupted?

_____

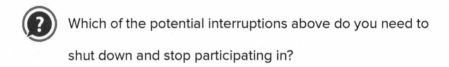 What specific apps and push notification applications do you need to remove from your smartphone to become more successful and to get more of your goals accomplished?

_____

MOVE #42

FIRE PEOPLE SUCCINCTLY BY SIMPLY
STATING, "IT'S NOT WORKING OUT."

NOTABLE QUOTABLE

"You have to be responsible when you're running an organization, and firing people who are your friends is part of that responsibility."

- BEN HOROWITZ

(He's an investor, blogger, and best-selling author. He co-founded the venture capital firm Andreessen Horowitz. He also co-founded and served the Chief Executive Officer of the enterprise software company Opsware, which Hewlett-Packard acquired for $1.6 billion in cash in July 2007.)

When it's time to fire someone, make it happen quickly, and don't get into a debate, a discussion or an ethics class with them. Simply tell the person you are firing: "It's not working out." Save yourself the next few hours of pointless dramatic conversations that you would have just invested in them. I would challenge you here and now to write out the answers to the following questions for your betterment:

? Who in your business needs to be fired for consistently not getting their job done?

_____

? Who in your business needs to be fired for having a bad attitude?

_____

? When is the most convenient time and place for you to fire them (I love firing people on Fridays)?

_____

MOVE #43

DON'T GO OUT TO DINNER WITH MORE
THAN 7 PEOPLE AT A TIME.

NOTABLE QUOTABLE

"If time be of all things the most precious,
wasting time must be the greatest prodigality."

- BENJAMIN FRANKLIN

*(The man that most historians consider to be one of the most intelligent men
in American history, yet he did rarely attended formal classes.
He spent two years of his life attending Boston Latin School and another
private academy before he decided that it would be a better use of his time
to join his family's candle business and soap manufacturing business. At the
age of 12 he began working a full-time apprentice for his brother James in a
printing business. Benjamin went on to found the University of
Pennsylvania and he actually received honorary degrees from Yale,
Harvard, Oxford, the College of William and Mary and the University
of St. Andrews.)*

When you go out to dinner with more than six people, you are going to witness two separate conversations that break out on either side of the table, and nobody will ever connect around one central conversation. When Doctor Zoellner first pointed out "The Rule of Six" to me, it astonished me how universally true it is. If you are going to attempt to connect with somebody over a meal for the purposes of business, you must not have more than 6 people involved in any meal or it will be unproductive. I would challenge you here and now to write out the answers to the following questions for your betterment:

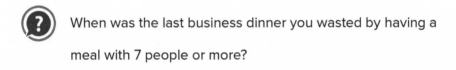 When was the last business dinner you wasted by having a meal with 7 people or more?

_____

When is the next business dinner you have scheduled?

_____

Is it possible to cut that guest list down to less than 6 people?

_____

MOVE #44

LET PEOPLE KNOW WHEN
YOUR CONVERSATION
HAS TO END BEFORE IT STARTS.

NOTABLE QUOTABLE

"Dost thou love life? Then do not squander time,
for that is the stuff life is made of."

- BENJAMIN FRANKLIN

(A man who became a celebrity author while still a teenager. When his brother James started a weekly newspaper called the New England Courant in the 1720s, Benjamin began writing and sending essays to the paper using the pen name of "Silence Dogood." This character was brilliant and the people in the community loved these essays. Ben wrote 14 essays the community found out that he was actually the now locally famous Mrs. Dogood. His brother did not like this and physically beat his brother. Benjamin, left Boston the following year to settle in Philadelphia, the city that became his new hometown for the remainder of his life.)

When you start a business conversation it's very important to state, "Hey, I'm glad we've scheduled this hour to get together...." or "Hey, I've got to pick up my kids at 5, but let's knock this out" or "Hey, I saw you called and I wanted to knock this out before heading into my last meeting."

I would challenge you here and now to write out the answers to the following questions for your betterment:

? Write down the "epic length quick call" people in your life that always have a way of morphing their "quick call" into a soul sucking hour of power?

_____

_____

_____

_____

Commit right here and now to stop having rabbit-trail and long-winded conversations with these "epic length quick call" people. You shouldn't feel like you are about to watch the movie Titanic every time you are talking to somebody.

MOVE #45

DESIGN YOUR SCHEDULE
IN LIFE SO THAT YOU CAN
MINIMIZE THE TIME YOU ARE
COMMUTING TO WORK.

NOTABLE QUOTABLE

"What we fear doing most is usually
what we most need to do."

- TIM FERRISS

*(In 2007, Tim released The 4-Hour Workweek which was published by crown,
a division of the famous Random House publishing house. Despite being
rejected by many publishers at first, it was a number 1 New York Times best
seller.)*

NOTABLE QUOTABLE

"Determine never to be idle. No person will have occasion to complain of the want of time who never loses any. It is wonderful how much can be done if we are always doing."

- THOMAS JEFFERSON

(One of the Founding Fathers of our country, who wrote the majority of the Declaration of Independence. He was the also the third President of the United States.)

One of our ThriveTimeShow.com mentors (teachers on the online school), was the first person to point out to me how much time people waste commuting to and from work which is why he chose to live nearby when he was the Executive Vice President of Operations for the a world famous theme park. My friend, if possible, find a way to reduce your commute to work. Do what you have to do to get that time back.

I would challenge you here and now to write out the answers to the following questions for your betterment:

Can you leave to work at a different time when the roads are less busy to reduce your commute time to work?

_____

Can you move closer to work to reduce your commute time to work?

_____

Could you move into the office (the first Walmart store manager that Sam Walton hired did this and so did Tony Hsieh the CEO of Zappos)?

_____

MOVE #46

TURN YOUR COMMUTE TO WORK INTO YOUR MOBILE CALL CENTER OR AUDIO SELF-HELP LIBRARY.

NOTABLE QUOTABLE

"The mind is what the mind is fed."

- DAVID J. SCHWARTZ

(The best-selling author of The Magic of Thinking Big.)

If you are going to have to drive to work, you might as well make your drive time productive or you might as well sell something. On my way home from work every day I am on the phone wrapping up the last calls of the day or closing a deal. On my way to work, every day, I am prepping my leadership team for the day and answering any questions they have about the upcoming day. You can do it.

I would challenge you here and now to write out the answers to the following questions for your betterment:

 What is one daily phone call that you could have in the car rather than at the office?

_____

 What is a daily podcast you could listen to while driving?
***Shameless plug: Check out the ThriveTimeShow.com business coach radio show and podcast today at www. ThriveTimeShow.com

_____

 What is a self-help audio book or auto-biography that you could be listening to on the way home?
***Recommendation: We recommend that every entrepreneur or aspiring entrepreneur listen to Think and Grow Rich by Napoleon Hill at least once.

_____

MOVE #47

SLEEP LESS. WORK MORE.

NOTABLE QUOTABLE

"By working only when you are most effective, life is both more productive and more enjoyable. It's the perfect example of having your
cake and eating it, too."

- TIM FERRISS

*(The best-selling author, investor and life-optimizer whose podcast The Tim
Ferriss Show has over 200+ million downloaded episodes.)*

....

There is so much discussion around being a workaholic or an
alcoholic, but nobody ever talks about being a sleep-a-holic and I
know specifically that one out of five people that I meet are struggling
sleep-a-holics. They have big dreams and ambitions but they lack the
self-discipline needed to get up and to get things done. If you are
allergic to coffee, I have a plan for you.

If you are against stimulants, I have a plan for you. If you are into
making excuses related to not having enough sleep for not getting

things done, but you refuse to heed the following advice, I encourage you write down all of your goals and dreams on a piece of paper before flushing that piece of paper down the toilet. It's not possible to be successful if you sincerely are unwilling to make a few trade-offs during your life for the success you want.

NOTABLE QUOTABLE

"This (the bi-phasic sleeping period) was probably one of the most productive periods of my life."

- MATT MULLENWEG

(The billionaire developer who developed the Wordpress Platform that nearly 20% of the internet is built on.)

FUN FACT: According to People Magazine, Matt Mullenweg's company (Automattic - which is the company behind WordPress) is currently worth over $1.16 billion) - The Hottest Billionaire Bachelors Worth Billions - People- http://people.com/archive/the-hottest-bachelors-worth-billions-vol-82-no-2/

 FUN FACT: To hear Tim Ferriss' interview with Matt Mullenweg where he discusses his bi-phasic sleeping patterns, visit the Four Hour Work Week Podcast at - https://tim.blog/2015/02/09/matt-mullenweg/. But, what if I am allergic to caffeine or I struggle to get myself going?

 FUN FACT: "Individuals need very different amounts of sleep. Though most of the population will survive pretty well on 7-8 hours of sleep (not bed time, sleep) per night, some do well on three hours, while others need nine. To start to figure this out, look at how much total sleep time you get on weekend and vacation days." - Psychology Today - https://www.psychologytoday.com/us/blog/the-power-rest/201009/how-much-sleep-do-i-need

My friend, if you struggle to get yourself going in the morning, I have both good and bad news for you. Here is a little secret: I also struggle with getting myself going, which is why I get myself going right away every morning by doing the following activities EVERY MORNING.

» **Step 1** - I listen to inspirational music to get me going.

» **Step 2** - I workout at 4 AM.

» **Step 3** - I create my to-do list before I interact with any other humans. This list sets the pace for how fast I will work during the day.

» **Step 4** - I attempt to stay hungry all day. For me personally I get tired after I eat and there is a massive quantity of scientific data that shows that most people get tired after a big meal. Thus, I eat very little during the day.

By design, I have been around enormously successful people for so long now, it's almost hard for me to empathize anymore with people who are unwilling to wake up early in exchange for the achievement of their dreams.

However, if you worked for me and you struggled to wake up, I would show you what I do every day to wake up, get going, and then I would encourage you to shut up and get moving. Don't be a mentally weak human, your future success is worth it.

I would challenge you here and now to write out the answers to the following questions for your betterment:

(?) How many hours of sleep do you truly need?

_____

(?) How many hours of sleep are you truly getting?

_____

(?) What are a few schedule changes that you are willing to implement in order to have higher quality sleep when you do sleep?

_____

.

MOVE #48

DRINK A MEAL REPLACEMENT SHAKE
AND DON'T EAT LUNCH.

NOTABLE QUOTABLE

"Lack of direction, not lack of time, is the problem.

We all have twenty-four hour days."

- ZIG ZIGLER

*(The New York Times best-selling author and
renowned motivational speaker.)*

When you are around enormously successful people, you will soon discover that the vast majority of them do not leave their office to each lunch. They would rather invest the 30 minutes they would normally spend commuting to and from lunch into doing something more productive. Well then what is one to eat? I encourage you to slam a meal replacement shake and to move on. I would challenge you here and now to write out the answers to the following questions for your betterment:

 What is some food that you could bring from home every day that would allow you to not have to leave office for lunch every day?

_____

 How much time per week does going to lunch currently cost you?

_____

MOVE #49

DON'T SPEND YOUR TIME LOOKING FOR SOMETHING TO WATCH (ON TV, NETFLIX, AMAZON, ETC.)

FUN FACT: "According to their findings, about 44 percent of Americans ages 16 to 69 spend an average of 23 minutes over the course of their day trying to pick something to watch. Extrapolating that number out over the roughly 80-year lifespan of the average American makes it 474 days, or 1.3 years." - American TV Watchers Spend Over a Year of Their Life Channel Surfing" - Danny Lewis - Smithsonian.com

Americans spend a staggering amount of time during their lifetimes looking for something to watch and this is before they invest an even more staggering amount of time watching TV. If you want to get more stuff done you need to watch MUCH LESS TV. Stop watching success stories on TV and invest your time into becoming one. Remember, as a general rule, rich people invest in big libraries and poor people invest in big TVs.

I would challenge you here and now to write out the answers to the following questions for your betterment:

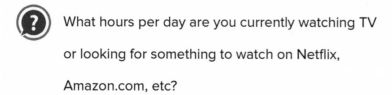 What hours per day are you currently watching TV or looking for something to watch on Netflix, Amazon.com, etc?

_____

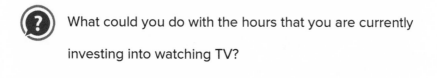 What could you do with the hours that you are currently investing into watching TV?

_____

MOVE #50

GATHER ALL OF THE FACTS AND
THEN ACT WITHOUT GATHERING THE
OPINIONS OF EVERYBODY ELSE.

NOTABLE QUOTABLE

"Successful people make decisions quickly (as soon as all
the facts are available) and change them very slowly (if ever).
Unsuccessful people make decisions very slowly,
and change them often and quickly."

- NAPOLEON HILL

*(The best-selling author of Think and Grow Rich and the man who President
Franklin Delano Roosevelt consulted with to help to help lift America out of
the Great Depression. Ever heard of "We have nothing to fear by fear itself?"
Guess who wrote that? Napoleon Hill.)*

The more success you begin to have the more unsolicited feedback, advice, and opinions you will begin to receive from others. If you begin to listen to all of the opinions from the left, center and right side of the aisle of life, you will never get anything done. There is always somebody who is "very worried that you are working too much," somebody that is telling you that, "you work too much," somebody who looks at everything from an emotional perspective, and somebody who thinks First Lady Michelle Obama is a man and that President George Bush blew up the towers himself so that we could "get their oil." Simply put, just gather the facts and act.

I would challenge you here and now to write out the answers to the following questions for your betterment:

 Who are the people in your life that are providing you with daily unsolicited feedback that is hindering your ability to get things done?

_____

 How can you minimize the number of people you have to run your decisions by before making life decisions that impact your overall quality of life and your ability to get things done?

_____

MOVE #51

WHEN YOU HEAR THE PHRASE
"COMMITTEE,"
RUN FOR THE HILLS.

NOTABLE QUOTABLE

"Opinions are the cheapest commodities on earth. Everyone has a flock of opinions ready to be wished upon anyone who will accept them. If you are influenced by "opinions" when you reach DECISIONS, you will not succeed in any undertaking."

- NAPOLEON HILL

(The best-selling author of Think and Grow Rich and the personal apprentice of the late great Andrew Carnegie.)

There is nothing more unproductive for most business situations than working with a committee of people to make a decision. This "task force" and "committee" will spend months playing "grab-ass" and going out to lunch. They will spend almost zero time gathering the facts and making the tough decisions. If you constantly feel the need to run everything in your life by a committee of people, you will lose in the game of life.

I would challenge you here and now to write out the answers to the following questions for your betterment:

 In what ways in your life are procrastinating on making decisions because you want to run your ideas by a massive committee of people?

_____

 What is a "grab-ass-playing" committee that you are currently serving on that you need to get off of?

_____

MOVE #52

DON'T SUFFER DEATH BY
"GOT-A-MINUTE" MEETINGS.

NOTABLE QUOTABLE

"Cut out the got-a-minute meetings and tell

employees to hold it for meeting."

- CHET HOLMES

(Best-selling author of The Ultimate Sales Machine.)

....

Super Moves: The Moves to Avoid the Got-A-Minute Meetings:

1. Observe the organizational chart

2. Encourage teammates to bring the questions up in the meeting

3. Pretend to be on a call

4. Pretend to be suffering an attack by a swarm of bees and run out the building yelling "Who let those bees in here!"

5. Fake an incoming call

6. Fake an injury

If you are going to be a productive and purposeful person, you are going to have to be focused and you can't remain focused when you are constantly interrupted.

In the world of small and medium-sized business, I have personally witnessed some of the most brilliant people reduced to the status of almost a zero-impact team player as a result of the constant barrage of "got-a-minute meetings." You have to work very hard to free yourself from these endless interruptions. I would challenge you here and now to write out the answers to the following questions for your betterment:

 How could you change the organization chart of your business to limit people's access to you? Who should people ask if they shouldn't ask you?

_____

 How could you change the structure or the frequency of your weekly meetings so that your team has a place and time to ask you their important questions all at once?

_____

How could you adjust your schedule to minimize your physical presence with your teammates so that it is now physically impossible for them to pelt you with unsolicited "got-a-minute" meeting questions?

_____

 What frequently asked question database could you create to provide a way for your teammates to get the answers to your questions without asking you for help?

_____

MOVE #53

PAY PEOPLE TO DO WHAT THEY DO BEST SO
YOU DON'T END UP SPENDING YOUR ENTIRE
DAY FIXING YOUR COMPUTER, CLEANING
YOUR HOUSE, DOING YOUR LAUNDRY
AND MOWING YOUR LAWN.

NOTABLE QUOTABLE

"If you spend your time, worth $20-25 per hour, doing something that someone else will do for $10 per hour, it's simply a poor use of resources."

- TIM FERRISS

(One of the world's leading authorities on time management and the best-selling author of The Four Hour Work Week series of books.)

Don't be greedy with money, especially when paying somebody to do a repetitive task that could save you massive amounts of time. For example, today I paid a company $78 to change my oil and it saved me 3 hours. I've been doing this kind of thing since I had three jobs and very little money working at Applebee's, Target and DirecTV. If I wanted to change my own oil, I would have had to have the skills, the equipment, and the physical space needed to change my oil. All of these things would have required time, which I cannot make more of. Today I'm not doing my laundry because I pay someone to do it and I'm not mowing my lawn because my son loves doing it. But, if my son wasn't passionate about mowing lawns, I would pay someone else to do it for me.

My friend you only live once, don't spend your entire day fixing your computer or cutting grass if you could be using that time to make more money than it costs you to pay someone to do it for you. You won't find a billionaire or anyone who is going to become a millionaire out there mowing their grass. Pay someone, when possible, to knock out life's tasks for you.

I would challenge you here and now to write out the answers to the following questions for your betterment:

 What are 3 tasks that you could hire someone to do for you so that you can buy back your time?

_____

 What is a piece of technology that you could invest in that could allow you to free up much of your time like buying a washing machine rather than sitting at a laundromat?

_____

MOVE #54

DON'T TRAVEL UNTIL YOU ARE NOT PERPETUALLY BEHIND.

NOTABLE QUOTABLE

"It's lonely at the top. Ninety-nine percent of people in the world are convinced they are incapable of achieving great things, so they aim for the mediocre. The level of competition is thus fiercest for 'realistic' goals, paradoxically making them the most time and energy-consuming."

- TIM FERRISS

(The best-selling self-help author of The 4-hour Work Week, The 4-hour Body, The 4-Hour Chef, and Tools of Titans.)

We all know people who travel all of the time for pleasure, but yet are perpetually behind at work, with their taxes, and with their lives in general. My friend, I would recommend that you do not travel until you are caught up and can stay that way. There is a season for everything, but I have seen way too many people trying to make this the "travel season of their life" while running around perpetually overwhelmed and behind. It's hard to get anything done if you are not physically present.

I would challenge you here and now to write out the answers to the following questions for your betterment:

 What systems or goals need to be accomplished before consistent traveling for pleasure can be reintroduced back into your life?

_____

 When was the last time you traveled for pleasure when you shouldn't have?

_____

MOVE #55

LIVE A PURPOSEFUL LIFE
BY CLEARLY KNOWING YOUR GOALS
AND PUTTING THEM INTO YOUR
SCHEDULE.

NOTABLE QUOTABLE

"For all their bitching about what's holding them back, most people have a lot of trouble coming up with the defined dreams they're being held from."

- TIM FERRISS

(An angel investor and an advisor to Facebook, Twitter, Evernote, and Uber, among other companies.)

....

We talked about it earlier during the book, but you have to know the purpose for your life and you must clearly define your F6 Goals if you are going to become a more productive person. You simply must invest the time to specifically map out the goals you have for your faith, family, friendships, fitness, finances, and fun or you will spend your time drifting around and not living the life you want. When you don't live purposefully and you allow yourself to drift you will LOSE BY DEFAULT.

I would challenge you here and now to write out the answers to the following questions for your betterment:

What are your specific one year goals for your faith?

_____

What are your specific one year goals for your family?

_____

What are your specific one year goals for your friendships?

_____

What are your specific one year goals for your fitness?

_____

What are your specific one year goals for your finances?

_____

What are your specific one year goals for your fun?

_____

What are your goals for how to stay successfully married?

_____

MOVE #56

DON'T ENGAGE IN GOSSIP.

NOTABLE QUOTABLE

"Do not let any unwholesome talk come out of your mouths, but only
what is helpful for building others up according to their needs, that it
may benefit those who listen."

- EPHESIANS 4:29

If possible, don't talk about people when they are not present. This is hard to do when you are in charge because often times you have to deal with nefarious employees and partners who are playing games and this requires strategizing. Also, as a leader, you must teach your next generation of people by examples and not abstract concepts, so occasionally, you must use real-life human examples. But as a general rule do not discuss other people when they are not present.

I would challenge you here and now to write out the answers to the following questions for your betterment:

 How could you minimize your discussions about the actions of other people in your life?

_____

 How could you minimize your discussion about the emotions of other people in your life?

_____

MOVE #57

DON'T OVER-COMMIT
TO THINGS.

NOTABLE QUOTABLE

"People think focus means saying yes to the thing you've got to focus on. But that's not what it means at all. It means saying no to the hundred other good ideas that there are. You have to pick carefully. I'm actually as proud of the things we haven't done as the things I have done. Innovation is saying no to 1,000 things."

- STEVE JOBS

(Co-founder of Apple and the former CEO of PIXAR who saved the company from a path of certain failure when he took over the company at the request of his dear friend, George Lucas.)

You don't have to do something just because someone asks you to. Thus, you don't need to feel the need to accept every dinner invitation, every calendar invite, and every request for a "quick meeting." If you feel like your current calendar is overwhelmed with obligations, then it is time to pull some over-commitment-weeds out of your calendar because they are choking off your life.

I would challenge you here and now to write out the answers to the following questions for your betterment:

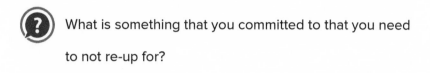 What is something that you committed to that you need to not re-up for?

_____

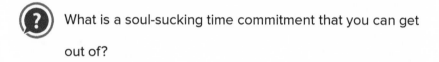 What is a soul-sucking time commitment that you can get out of?

_____

What is an association or networking club that you need to get out of?

_____

MOVE #58

CREATE A CHECKLIST FOR EVERYTHING.

NOTABLE QUOTABLE

"We don't like checklists. They can be painstaking. They're not much fun. But I don't think the issue here is mere laziness. There's something deeper, more visceral going on when people walk away not only from saving lives but from making money. It somehow feels beneath us to use a checklist, an embarrassment. It runs counter to deeply held beliefs about how the truly great among us—those we aspire to be—handle situations of high stakes and complexity. The truly great are daring. They improvise. They do not have protocols and checklists. Maybe our idea of heroism needs updating."

- ATUL GAWANDE

(The surgeon, writer, and public health researcher who is a professor in the Department of Health Policy and Management at the Harvard T.H. Chan School of Public Health and the Samuel O. Their Professor of Surgery at Harvard Medical School. He is the best-selling author of The Checklist Manifesto.)

NOTABLE QUOTABLE

"The volume and complexity of what we know has exceeded our individual ability to deliver its benefits correctly, safely, or reliably (without a checklist)."

- ATUL GAWANDE

(The surgeon, writer, and public health researcher who is a professor in the Department of Health Policy and Management at the Harvard T.H. Chan School of Public Health and the Samuel O. Their Professor of Surgery at Harvard Medical School. He is the best-selling author of
The Checklist Manifesto.)

Southwest Airlines uses checklists for maintaining and flying planes, Manhattan Construction uses checklists for buildings, Starbucks uses checklists for cleaning their bathrooms, Wholefoods uses checklists for their daily operations, and basically anything that is consistently of high quality involves the use of a checklist. Thus, if you want to have a high-quality vacation, office, or life, use a checklist.

I would challenge you here and now to write out the answers to the following questions for your betterment:

? In what areas of life would a checklist save you massive amounts of time and potential forgetfulness?

_____

? How many sales are you losing as a result of forgetting to follow-up?

_____

? When was the last trip you went on where you forgot to bring underwear, pants, a tie, or something important because you didn't have a packing checklist?

_____

MOVE #59

DON'T CHASE NEW IDEAS AND
BUSINESSES UNTIL YOU ARE
CURRENTLY SUCCEEDING WITH
YOUR FIRST IDEA OR BUSINESS.

NOTABLE QUOTABLE

"Concentrate all your thoughts upon the work at hand.

The sun's rays do not burn until brought to a focus."

- SIR ISAAC NEWTON

(The mathematician, astronomer, and physicist who many consider to be one of the most influential scientists of all time.)

Aspiring entrepreneurs, lovers, and car buyers all love "the new one," because it's new. People love their new girlfriend, her incredible laugh, and the way she walks. Oh, everyone loves the new car, and they have a blasty blast hopping inside of it, giving the new car a fabulous sniffy sniff so that they can enjoy the new car smell. People love their newest business idea best because it's their best idea ever. Never mind that their current business is barely surviving. It is actually failing because their new idea is going to be so amazing it will more than makeup for the losses on their previous ventures. This gambler's mindset to chronically chase new ideas and new lovers will lead you down the path to poverty, but at least you will have a bunch of upset stepchildren, bitter partners, and massive car payments to show for it.

I would challenge you here and now to write out the answers to the following questions for your betterment:

 In what way have you been guilty of chasing the new idea, the new business or the new something?

_____

 Will you commit here and now to stop chasing new ideas until you execute your current ideas.

_____

MOVE #60

DON'T SCALE IT UNTIL
YOU NAIL IT.

NOTABLE QUOTABLE

"Truth is ever to be found in simplicity, and not in the multiplicity and confusion of things."

- SIR ISAAC NEWTON

(The mathematician, astronomer, and physicist who made many of his most profound discoveries while still technically a college student. In 1665 The Great Plague ravaged England and Cambridge was closed and the students were forced to seek refuge in the countryside. During this time Isaac Newton began refining his theories on light, color, calculus, and gravity. He even built the first reflecting microscope in 1668.)

I often meet entrepreneurs who want to open up location #3 of their business before location #2 is profitable. I meet other entrepreneurs who want to "franchise their proven system" that is consistently losing money for them. My friend you must nail it and get the system correct and profitable before you attempt to scale it.

I would challenge you here and now to write out the answers to the following questions for your betterment:

(?) **In what ways does your system have to improve before you can scale it?**

_____

_____

_____

_____

_____

_____

_____

_____

_____

What goals or metrics of success will you have to see before you know that it is time to scale the business?

_____

_____

_____

_____

_____

_____

_____

_____

_____

_____

_____

_____

_____

_____

MOVE #61

DON'T NETWORK AT EVENTS WHERE POTENTIAL CLIENTS ARE NOT PRESENT, AND WHERE VAPING AND CHRONICALLY DIVORCED PEOPLE SPEND THEIR TIME MAKING BASELESS CLAIMS ABOUT GOD-FEARING PATRIOTS.

NOTABLE QUOTABLE

"You are the average of the five people you associate with most, so do not underestimate the effects of your pessimistic, unambitious, or disorganized friends. If someone isn't making you stronger, they're making you weaker."

- TIM FERRISS

(The best-selling author of The 4-Hour Workweek and an early investor in Facebook, Uber and other massively successful companies.)

We've all found ourselves in someone's living room or at some networking event surrounded by people that you know don't have a snowball's chance in hell of becoming a potential customer. Yet, you are there investing your time. If you are recruiting to find the next super rapper, stop going to NASCAR events and country music dance halls. If you want to get more stuff done during your typical work day, you just have to be realistic.

I would challenge you here and now to write out the answers to the following questions for your betterment:

 In what ways are you fishing in the lake for a horse?

_____

 In what ways are you wasting your time networking?

_____

MOVE #62

DON'T DRIVE AROUND LOOKING TO
SAVE TWO CENTS PER GALLON ON GAS

NOTABLE QUOTABLE

"Information is useless if it is not applied to something important

or if you will forget it before you have a chance to apply it."

- TIM FERRISS

*(The best-selling author of the The 4-Hour Workweek the number one
position on the New York Times bestseller list, No. 1 on The Wall Street
Journal bestseller list, and No. 1 on the BusinessWeek bestseller list.
The book currently sold over 1,350,000 copies and spent nearly 4
years on the New York Times bestseller list.)*

In the event that you do save those 2 cents per gallon and you are driving a boat to work every day, you saved a massive $1.00 (if you bought 50 gallons of gas). Then as you drive your boat to work (assuming that your boat gets 20 miles per gallon) you will soon do the mental math to discover that the 3 miles you drove to save those 2 cents per gallon has quickly been negated by the fact it cost you all that time to only save $1 on the cost of filling up your boat.

I would challenge you here and now to write out the answers to the following questions for your betterment:

 Get out your finger, prick it and sign it in blood. Henceforth, I will not drive around for miles and miles to save 2 cents per gallon on the price of gas.

      a. Name _____

      b. Date _____

MOVE #63

TAKE THE CUMULATIVE TIME THAT YOU WOULD SPEND DOING POINTLESS NETWORKING AND DRIVING AROUND LOOKING FOR GAS AND READ THE FOLLOWING 8 BOOKS THAT HAVE THE POWER TO CHANGE YOUR MINDSET WHICH WILL CHANGE YOUR LIFE.

I would challenge you here and now to write out the answers to the following questions for your betterment:

 Why don't you have the time needed to read the books that have the power to change your life? _____

_____

_____

 When will you begin reading the following books?

_____

» **Book #1** - *Start Here: The World's Best Business Growth & Consulting Book: Business Growth Strategies from the World's Best Business Coach* by me (Clay Clark)

» **Book #2** - *Think and Grow Rich* by Napoleon Hill

» **Book #3** - *How to Win Friends and Influence People* by Dale Carnegie

» **Book #4** - *Soft-Selling in a Hard World* by Jerry Vass

» **Book #5** - *The Service Profit Chain* by James L. Heskett and W. Earl Sasser

» **Book #6** - *The Purple Cow* by Seth Godin

» **Book #7** - *Winning* by Jack Welch

» **Book #8** - *Boom* by me (Clay Clark)

MOVE #64

DON'T LET PROBLEM
EMPLOYEES PERPETUATE THEIR POOR
PERFORMANCE.

NOTABLE QUOTABLE

"Poisonous people do not deserve your time.

To think otherwise is masochistic."

- TIM FERRISS

(The personality behind one of the top podcasts on the planet.)

If you have a poor performer on your team, they are going to irritate your clients and customers to the point that they will fire you if you do not fire them. Thus, fire poor performing employees as soon as possible. YOU MUST DO THIS BEFORE THE CUSTOMER FIRES YOU.

I would challenge you here and now to write out the answers to the following questions for your betterment:

 Who on your team needs to be punted?

_____

 Who on your team have you let poison your culture and your customer base to avoid having that one "tough discussion?"

_____

MOVE #65

DON'T PROMOTE YOUR SEXUAL
PARTNER TO BECOME THE HEAD OF
YOUR COMPANY JUST BECAUSE
YOU'RE INFATUATED WITH THEM AND
LOVE HAVING SEX WITH THEM.

NOTABLE QUOTABLE

"People around you, constantly under the pull of their emotions, change their ideas by the day or by the hour, depending on their mood. You must never assume that what people say or do in a particular moment is a statement of their permanent desires."

- ROBERT GREENE

(The best-selling author who has written five international bestselling books, including: The 48 Laws of Power, The Art of Seduction, The 33 Strategies of War, The 50th Law (with rapper 50 Cent), and Mastery.)

Oh the awkwardness of writing this and reading this, but it's true and we all know it. You know it. I know it, and they know we know it. Everybody knows that you promoted this person to be in charge of your company because you love having sex with them. Don't do it. I promise that their ability to score high in sexual gymnastics has nothing do with their ability to perform at work.

I would challenge you here and now to write out the answers to the following questions for your betterment:

Who have you promoted to a level of incompetence because you or someone is having sex with them?

_____

Who is still in charge of something because you or someone else once had sex with them?

_____

BONUS FRIES
(SUPER SALTY SUPER MOVES THAT YOU CAN USE TO GET MORE THINGS DONE):

The comedian Jim Gaffigan once pointed out that we've all guiltily enjoyed the pleasure of finishing a large order of McDonald's fries only to discover a miracle at the bottom of the bag. When we find that unexpected bonus French fry just waiting to be eaten after we thought for sure that there was no more goodness to be had. My friend, behold! The bonus fry super salty super moves that you can use to free up more time in your schedule and to get more stuff done. Because they are salty.

1. Hang up on people when needed.

When you are talking to someone on the phone and you know that the conversation is going nowhere you may want to think about hanging up after your tactful attempts to end the conversation are obviously not working. Once you have firmly established in your mind that you are never going to need to talk to this person again, politely try to wrap up the conversation two more times.

If they don't get it, I encourage you to hang up and to enjoy the next 2 minutes of "free-time" knowing that you are not spending that time on the phone talking to your angry ex-girlfriend, an ex-employee, an ex-family member, an ex-high-pressure-salesperson-acquaintance or the woman at the Elephant In The Room who continues to want to get her haircut at the men's only grooming lounge.

I would challenge you here and now to write out the answers to the following questions for your betterment:

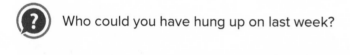 Who could you have hung up on last week?

_____

 Who could you hang up on this week?

_____

2. Pull an all-nighter for something that must get done.

Many times throughout my career I have discovered that there is simply not enough time to get a task done unless I stay up all night while working without ceasing. So, that is exactly what I have done. As our businesses have grown and dramatically increased, the number of highly-skilled team members that I can confidently delegate to the need for all-nighters has almost completely disappeared, but I have pulled "all-nighters" countless times throughout my career. I have found that when you are passionate about something the concept of pulling an "all-nighter" is not so daunting or terrible. In fact, science has shown that when you are completely mentally and physically immersed in doing something you actually experience a mental state known as "flow state" where you lose track of both space and time.

For example, when I am writing music, book writing, workflow designing, mixing music, writing cold-call scripts or pro-creating with my wife I am in the "flow state" (which is why I have five kids). Why do I have to write these awkward things? You'll remember this principle longer.

FUN FACT: "To find out what's going on in the brain when we remember certain things and forget others, the scientists had volunteers memorize that a specific word was linked with two different, unrelated pictures. To remember that the word "sand" was linked with an image of Marilyn Monroe, for example, someone might picture Marilyn on a sandy beach. Then, to remember that "sand" was also linked with a hat, someone might think of the hat covered in sand.

Every time the volunteers linked a specific image with a word, they formed a distinct pattern in the area of the brain responsible for storing visual information.

The researchers came up with a way to identify each of these patterns (let's call them the "Marilyn pattern," for example, and the "hat pattern") on a computer. After the volunteers had linked both images with the word, the researchers told them they only had to worry about remembering the first one.

Next, they took the volunteers to another room, where the word "sand" was being flashed occasionally on a blank screen. At first, the volunteers' brains displayed both the Marilyn pattern and the hat pattern when they saw the word. But over time, the hat pattern grew dim while the Marilyn pattern stayed clear. In other words, the volunteers were remembering the image of Marilyn by discarding the image of the hat. "It's the brain's way of keeping everything that's up to date, and telling the rest it can go," University of Birmingham psychology professor and the study's lead author Maria Wimber told Business Insider. "Scientists have finally figured out why we remember some things and forget others." - Erin Brodwin - Business Insider

 FUN FACT: In positive psychology, "flow", also known as the zone, is the mental state of operation in which a person

performing an activity is fully immersed in a feeling of energized focus, full involvement, and enjoyment in the process of the activity. In essence, "flow" is characterized by complete absorption in what one does, and a resulting loss in one's sense of space and time.

I would challenge you here and now to write out the answers to the following questions for your betterment:

? What is something game-changing on your to-do list that has been lingering that you could really knock out if you just invested one "all-nighter" into completing this task?

_____

? When was the last time you invested an "all-nighter" into chasing your spouse around?

_____

*Quick Note: I'm a zealot for marital sex because apparently nobody else is.

NOTABLE QUOTABLE

"The all-nighter at the laboratory must have been a routine occurrence, for the discovery was treated surprisingly casually in the lab's notebooks."

- THE WIZARD OF MENLO PARK BY RANDALL STROSS

(the book written about Thomas Edison's prolific career as an inventor.)

....

3. Don't invite non-essential team members to meetings.

We've all found ourselves in a meeting that we didn't need to be in and that we really shouldn't have to be in. Just because someone is your partner, your spouse, an employee or a teammate doesn't mean you have to invite them into every meeting.

NOTABLE QUOTABLE

"A man has no right to waste another man's time and to rob his fellow man of his most important asset (his time)."

- CLAY CLARK

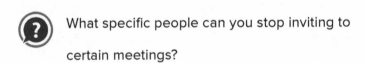

I would challenge you here and now to write out the answers to the following questions for your betterment:

What specific people can you stop inviting to certain meetings?

_____

What are specific meetings that you don't need to attend?

_____

DEEP THOUGHT - Upon further review, I believe that most of the college classes I attended were a waste of time and large expensive meetings that we didn't need to be in:

 Quantitative literacy - My vast knowledge of how to chart a slope on a graph has never been used in business.

 Humanities - My mastery and memorization of the magnificent achievements of Mesopotamian River valley men and women have never been used in the world of business.

 Psychology 101 - My understanding of the Electra complex has never been used to solve complex business problems and it's just weird.

4. Don't read messages until you are in a place to deal with them immediately.

Don't check your text messages, your emails, your voicemails or open your office mail until you are in a place where you can deal with them immediately. Last night I took my daughter to The Olive Garden with her friends to celebrate her 13th birthday.

There my mental capacity and critical thinking skills were reduced to that of the average buttery breadstick.

Something about being in a packed restaurant, surrounded by hundreds of people, with constant interruption by our server asking if I want more soup, the guy next to me talking loudly about some work grievance, teenage girls having a great time talking loudly about teenage girl stuff, the battle of keeping my 10 year old son from having 14 breadsticks, and having "Come Fly with Me" by Frank Sinatra on surround sound, made it impossible for me to check my phone messages. Stop checking your messages at The Olive Garden, while on dates, or at your kid's soccer game.

Stop checking messages in the bathroom, it's weird and it freaks me out every time I see you holding your phone up to your ear after having seen you use your smartphone while peeing at the urinal (ladies I apologize for this reference, but men need this DEEP higher-level education).

Men, there is simply no reason to be urinating while conversing on the phone. You must choose to make the call or to aim your...

I would challenge you here and now to write out the answers to the following questions for your betterment:

When did you most recently check messages in a place where you were not able to respond appropriately (emails in the bathroom)?

_____

 What places and times do you need to stop checking messages?

_____

5. Address concerns as immediately as possible.

We've all been mad about something and let it fester. This is not a move, yet we've all done it. In fact, as an example, my brother is a person I don't like and I am person that he does not like. However, he had some issues with my father that he decided to not bring up until my Dad's actual funeral after his tragic death after losing his long battle with ALS.

Thus, in front of all of my Dad's family and friends and at the burial site he decides to air his grievances at the actual funeral. Thus, I physically assaulted him and thus I had to go to court for punching him in the face. Thus, I had to pay my incredible attorney Wes Carter with Winters and King to represent me in court.

The moral of the story, if you have a problem with your father tell him while he is laying on the bed and can't physically go anywhere, don't wait until after he is dead and can't defend himself or your brother will knock you the F$%& out!

I would challenge you here and now to write out the answers to the following questions for your betterment:

 Who do you need to forgive for your betterment?

_____

 Who do you need to deal with now so that you don't have a lingering issue in your life?

_____

6. Put your phone on Do Not Disturb.

Nothing is worse that watching you try to check messages in meetings or at work while you're trying to look like you are not trying to check messages at work. You slick person you. She sees you checking your emails underneath the table while you're at The Olive Garden. Oh he sees you checking your emails at church. Oh yes. We all see you checking your emails at your workstation while pretending you are not. Don't be an idiot, just turn your phone onto the do-not-disturb mode so that you can actually be physically and mentally present.

I would challenge you here and now to write out the answers to the following questions for your betterment:

 What are consistent activities and places where you need to turn your do-not disturb feature on?

_____

 When was the last time you got in trouble with your significant other for not being mentally present... like responding to emails during dinner when you are out to eat?

_____

NOTABLE QUOTABLE

"If you love life, don't waste time.

For time is what life is made of."

- BRUCE LEE

(The famous Hong Kong actor, American actor, film director, and martial arts instructor.)

NOTABLE QUOTABLE

"There is nothing less productive than to make

more efficient what should not be done at all."

- PETER DRUCKER

(Known by Business leaders as the
"Founder of modern management".)

MOVE #66

STOP GETTING DIVORCED.

MOVE #67

STOP VAPING.

MOVE #68

STOP VOTING FOR OBAMA.

CPSIA information can be obtained
at www.ICGtesting.com
Printed in the USA
BVHW082225041122
651243BV00006B/152

9 780999 864906